PORTFOLIO / PENGUIN

GOOD ADVICE
FROM BAD PEOPLE

Zac Bissonnette is the *New York Times* bestselling author of *How to Be Richer, Smarter, and Better-Looking Than Your Parents* and *Debt-Free U*. He also edited the 2013 edition of the *Warman's Guide to Antiques and Collectibles* and has written for *Boston Globe Magazine*, *The Wall Street Journal*, *The Daily Beast*, and Bloomberg.com. He is currently working on a book about the story of the Beanie Babies mania of the 1990s and Ty Warner, the tycoon behind the craze.

In late 2013 he was blocked on Twitter by Donald Trump.

GOOD

FROM BAD PEOPLE

ADVICE

Selected Wisdom from Murderers, Stock Swindlers, and Lance Armstrong

ZAC BISSONNETTE

PORTFOLIO / PENGUIN

PORTFOLIO / PENGUIN
Published by the Penguin Group
Penguin Group (USA) LLC
375 Hudson Street
New York, New York 10014

USA | Canada | UK | Ireland | Australia
New Zealand | India | South Africa | China
penguin.com
A Penguin Random House Company

First published by Portfolio / Penguin, a member of Penguin
Group (USA) LLC, 2014

ISBN 978-1-59184-689-5

Printed in the United States of America
1 3 5 7 9 10 8 6 4 2

Set in Gotham
Designed by Alissa Rose Theodor

A portion of the proceeds from every book sold will be used to purchase mass-produced consumer goods for the author.

CONTENTS

CONTENTS

INTRODUCTION

WHERE SHALL WISDOM
BE FOUND?

Welcome to the first page of the last self-help book you'll ever want to buy.

Americans love self-help. In 2008, even at the height of the recession, we spent eleven billion dollars on self-improvement products—13.6 percent more than in 2005, when we were spending money on everything from sub-prime mortgages to Ashlee Simpson CDs. No matter how bad the world was, and how much evidence there was that it was all spinning out of our control, we still believed that strangers smiling at us from the covers of their own books could make our lives better.

But all too often, America's smiling, inspirational prophets turn out to be comically—and sometimes darkly—horrible at following their own leads: A guy writes a book on how to build "instant rapport" with strangers—and then gets arrested for threatening a receptionist. Lance Armstrong preaches about winning with integrity. Donald Trump warns about the pitfalls of narcissism. These kinds of charlatans rise to the top because, in our desperate need for motivational figures, we make almost no effort to vet them.

It's tempting to dismiss these people as frauds—hypocritical mountebanks who cashed in without regard to their own failings. Some of these guys—and yes, they are almost without exception guys—are just that.

But there's another, more charitable explanation for this unbelievable contradiction between the advice people give and the things people do. Freud called it "psychological projection." Historian Peter Gay defines projection as "the operation of expelling feelings or wishes the individual finds wholly unacceptable—too shameful, too obscene, too dangerous—by attributing them to another." The people who think that others would benefit from a book advising them not to resort to violence to solve problems are often exactly the kind of people who hire ex-cons to kill their stepdaughter's high school principal (see page 106). Still, good advice abounds, and there are enough examples to fill up a book that will improve your life as much as any other collection of self-help quotes—as long as you can follow it better than the people who gave it. It's not enough to know what to do or to be able to phrase it eloquently: if you want to be a compassionate man, don't assault a flight attendant because the grapes arrived prepackaged with the cheese (see page 125).

A NOTE ON SOURCES: The biographical material on each Bad Person was culled from reputable media outlets and is, to the best of the author's knowledge, accurate. In the case of criminal matters, please remember that all suspects are innocent until proven guilty.

PART ONE

MONEY SECRETS (E.G., THE PEOPLE WHO WROTE THESE BOOKS HAVE NO MONEY)

The past fifteen years have led to the unmasking of more financial "geniuses" than any period in U.S. history. It started with Enron around the turn of the millennium but really heated up in 2009 with the financial crisis in full swing, and with Bernie Madoff, Teresa Giudice, and dozens of others.

While the details vary, the roots of the falls are usually the same: shortsighted obsession with reward at the expense of risk management, arrogant overconfidence, and eagerness to suspend disbelief.

Naturally though, the word on Wall Street has always been long-term growth, discretion, and reliability; the most successful entrepreneurs and investors certainly personify those ideals, but those ideals' most vocal proponents often don't.

It is better and less expensive to avoid getting ill than it is to treat an existing illness. In a similar way, it is better and less expensive to organize your affairs so that you will not need to go to court than it is to go to court and win.

—Sonny Bloch, *Sonny Bloch's Cover Your Assets*

Sonny Bloch was that rare guru who did follow his own advice—in this case about avoiding court appearances at all costs. A lounge singer turned popular syndicated talk-radio host in the 1980s and early '90s (he once had Alan Greenspan on as a guest), Bloch used his radio platform to peddle all manner of dubious investments, including gold bars that were actually spray-painted metal and stakes in Venezuelan radio stations—almost always without disclosing to listeners that he was the one on the other side of the trade. When first-time callers but longtime listeners at the Justice Department, IRS, and Securities and Exchange Commission came bearing indictments and lawsuits, Bloch fled to the Dominican Republic, where his wife owned property—the ultimate litigation avoidance strategy. He was extradited in 1995, served two years at Club Fed, and was freed after he was found to be suffering from late-stage lung cancer; the prosecutor requested his release after Bloch told him he believed the cancer was divine retribution for his crimes. He died in 1998 at the age of sixty-one.

The only barriers in your career
are self-imposed.

—Albert J. Dunlap, *Mean Business:
How I Save Bad Companies and
Make Good Companies Great*

In the early- to mid-1990s, no one personified the archetype of the tough, take-no-prisoners CEO quite like Al Dunlap. He proudly went by the nickname Chainsaw Al, and his pink slip–heavy turnaround of Scott Paper made him an icon of everything America needed to stay competitive in the twenty-first century. In July 1996, Sunbeam announced that it had hired him as CEO, and the stock soared 50 percent in one day; 1996's *Mean Business*, his guide to management strategies, was an instant *New York Times* bestseller.

These days, though, the main barrier to Dunlap's career isn't exactly self-imposed: in 2002, to settle civil fraud charges brought by the SEC, Dunlap agreed to never serve as an officer or director of a public company for the rest of his goddamn life (as Dunlap, who was fond of screaming obscenities at subordinates, might have put it). The SEC estimated that at least sixty million dollars of Sunbeam's 1997 profits were fraudulent, and the company fell into bankruptcy under the weight of the ill-fated acquisitions Dunlap had engineered to mask the company's failing financial health. After Sunbeam, *New York Times* reporters uncovered similar misdeeds at his past turnaround efforts.

John A. Byrne, a *BusinessWeek* reporter who authored a book on Dunlap's rise and fall, summarized his career this way: "In all my years of reporting, I had never come across an executive as manipulative, ruthless, and destructive as Al Dunlap. . . . Dunlap sucked the very life and soul out of companies and people. He stole dignity, purpose, and sense out of organizations and replaced those ideals with fear and intimidation."

I began my career as something of a conservative when it came to finances, believing that simply by conserving cash in accounts that provided compound interest one possessed a very powerful tool in building wealth. I still believe in those principles today, 30 years later, only now I am pushing it to the next level.

—Anthony Cutaia, *Untapped Riches: Never Pay Off Your Mortgage—and Other Surprising Secrets for Building Wealth*

The gem on the previous page is sound advice—the only sound advice in the entire book. For Cutaia, trouble started when people questioned exactly whose cash was in those accounts.

Published in 2007, *Untapped Riches* is a sort of time capsule of just how moronic the conventional wisdom about things such as debt and real estate got during the real estate bubble. With chapter titles like "The Single Worst Mortgage in Creation: The Fixed Rate Mortgage" and "Negative Amortization: A Mouthful of a Phrase, a Generator of Quick Cash," this book is not only Cutaia's swan song but quite possibly the worst personal finance book ever written. Where most others are merely vapid, *Untapped Riches* contains advice that, if followed, would ruin your life; indeed, the year his book came out, Cutaia filed for bankruptcy. He had filed in 1994 as well.

But the real excitement came a few years later.

In January 2012, Mr. Cutaia was sentenced to fifty-one months in prison for soliciting investments from more than a dozen people and then using the proceeds for vacations, gambling, and loan repayment. One of his mistakes? Conning Palm Beach Gardens police chief Stephen Stepp, who called Cutaia an "unbelievable scammer" at the sentencing. All told, Cutaia stole about 1.5 million dollars from investors who trusted him based on his radio show, frequent seminars, and book signings; Cutaia blamed his crimes on his bipolar disorder. He's scheduled to be released from federal prison in 2015.

If you'll do for a few years what most people won't do, you'll be able to do for the rest of your life what most people can't do.

—Wade Cook, *Wade Cook's Power Quotes*

In Mr. Cook's case, "what most people won't do" included obstructing justice and neglecting to report $9.5 million of income from the sale of his books, tapes, and seminars.

Cook, a former cabdriver who often spoke of his humble roots in his seminars and ubiquitous radio commercials, used a slew of interlocking corporations and nonprofits to try to hide income from the authorities. According to a Motley Fool report, "Prosecutors charge that Cook and his wife set up a fraudulent charitable trust and limited partnership, ostensibly to benefit the Mormon Church, that instead funneled money to them. They ended up buying Arabian show horses, his-and-hers Cadillac Escalades, and a 40-acre estate. According to the charges, the Cooks were able to declare taxable royalties of just $980 in 1998, when in reality they received almost $5 million."

These days, at sixty-four years old, Cook has a scheduled release date of January 22, 2015, from the medium-security Federal Correctional Institution in Sheridan, Oregon. In the meantime, he is doing something else most people won't ever do: looking forward to a day when he can take a shit without having to ask his cellie to give him some privacy.

You have to be confident as you face the world each day, but you can't be too cocky. Anyone who thinks he's going to win them all is going to wind up a huge loser.

—Donald Trump, *Trump: Surviving at the Top*

Poets couldn't make up such irony: advice on humility from a guy whose empire was collapsing under the weight of excessive debt borne of grandiosity. Post-collapse and restructuring, Trump reinvented himself as a made-for-TV mogul.

Even his financial downfall didn't inspire Trump to take his own advice about cockiness; his 2004 book was the ambitiously titled *Trump: Think Like a Billionaire: Everything You Need to Know About Success, Real Estate, and Life*—yet another *New York Times* bestseller.

If you're not afraid to ask why, you can change whatever it is you want.

—Enron commercial

Enron is the only nonperson to make this book, which is fitting: after the company imploded under the weight of accounting fraud, no one at the top seemed to have had anything to do with it personally—it was just Enron, they told Congress. No one person had been involved.

Enron was, throughout the 1990s and into the early 2000s, one of the most admired companies in America. The company had started as a boring natural gas company but had transformed itself into an exciting Internet/technology/trading behemoth. It was considered a haven for the smartest workers, and *Fortune* magazine named it the Most Innovative Company in America for six years running—from 1995 through 2000.

"Ask Why" was Enron's slogan for a few years, but when an analyst had the audacity to ask why the company couldn't produce a balance sheet to go with its quarterly results like every other public company did, CEO Jeff Skilling responded by calling the analyst an "asshole." Skilling's lieutenants saluted him with a banner in the office that read "Ask why, asshole." A few months later Enron went bankrupt and when prosecutors started asking why, they quickly arrested most of the company's top executives and charged them with changing whatever it was that they had wanted to—in this case, financial results.

The other good thing about having money is that you can give it away. One of the things I care most about is trying to give as many kids as possible the same kind of opportunities I had.

—Evander Holyfield, *Becoming Holyfield*

Holyfield—who didn't meet his own father until he was twenty-one—did indeed manage to provide his kids with the same opportunities he had: the opportunity to grow up without a responsible father.

A dedicated Christian who mentioned God around forty times in a three-minute interview after pummeling the crap out of Mike Tyson, Holyfield has eleven children with six women. In 2012, he was held in contempt of court for failing to pay more than a half million dollars in back child support. That same year he went into foreclosure on his fourteen-million-dollar mansion.

Holyfield earned well over fifty million dollars during his career, but his own lavish lifestyle left little to fulfill his obligations to his progeny.

As an impresario, I encourage
and elicit contrarian views and
contrasts. We want people to be
able to see more than they
ordinarily might. . . . I find the
process of reaching a decision
more valuable than the results.
It's important to place tension
between points of view to extract
the best from people. Dissent
stimulates discussion, prompting
others to make more perceptive
observations.

—John Sculley, *Odyssey: Pepsi to Apple. . .
A Journey of Adventure, Ideas and the Future*

In May 1985, Apple's new CEO, John Sculley, learned that Steve Jobs, the company's founder, thought that Scully was "bad for Apple" and was planning to try to get him fired. Sculley went to the board of directors to complain about the insubordinate visionary—and won. When Sculley placed tension between himself and Jobs, he extracted the worst from the situation. They stripped Jobs of all his management responsibilities, and five months later Jobs left the company that he had built out of nothing.

Two years later, Sculley released his own memoir-cum-management guide. The flap copy promised a book that "offers advice on such topics as . . . how to manage creative people and how to invent the future." *The New York Times* called the book "severely overwritten," and there is, perhaps, a lesson for investors in it: If your company's CEO has time to author a severely overwritten book on how to be an incredible executive, it may perhaps be time to sell the stock; if your CEO refers to himself as an impresario repeatedly in that book, short the stock.

In 1993, following years of disappointing results, Apple's board of directors pushed Sculley out. A few years later, Steve Jobs, the man who Sculley had fired for his contrarian views, came back and eventually turned Apple into the world's most profitable company. And he did it all without publishing a self-serving autohagiography.

If an investment seems too good
to be true, it probably is. Don't fall
prey to get-rich-quick schemes.
Stick with those time-proven ways
to grow your nest egg.

—*The Beardstown Ladies'*
Little Book of Investment Wisdom

Ah, the 1990s. The stock market was riding high and with that came the democratization of investing; online brokers made it so anyone could trade, and the Beardstown Ladies—an investment club formed by a group of friends in Beardstown, Illinois—scored a mega-bestselling book with *The Beardstown Ladies' Common-Sense Investment Guide: How We Beat the Stock Market—and How You Can, Too*. "23.4% Annual Return" blared the cover, and the first paragraph of the dust jacket bragged that they had beaten professional money managers by a ratio of three to one. The pitch was perfect for talk shows: a group of old, badly dressed women who made more money investing than sophisticated financial advisors and hedge funds with armies of researchers.

That book's success (800,000 copies sold) led to mega-royalties and, of course, endless spin-offs: *The Beardstown Ladies' Pocketbook Guide to Picking Stocks*, *The Beardstown Ladies' Little Book of Investment Wisdom*, *The Beardstown Ladies' Guide to Smart Spending for Big Savings: How to Save for a Rainy Day Without Sacrificing Your Lifestyle*, and *The Beardstown Ladies' Stitch-in-Time Guide to Growing Your Nest Egg: Step-by-Step Planning for a Comfortable Financial Future*. There was also a VHS: *The Beardstown Ladies: Cookin' Up Profits on Wall Street—A Guide to Common Sense Investing*.

Unfortunately, the ladies' had miscalculated their returns—including their monthly contributions to their portfolio as investment gains. When their returns were calculated properly by a professional, it turned out they had actually lagged the indices they claimed to be beating—achieving 9 percent, not the 23 percent they'd advertised. Hyperion, the ladies' publisher, pulled the books out of print and offered exchanges as part of the settlement of a class-action lawsuit. The Beardstown investment club continues its meetings—although the ladies would probably be better off if they'd just put their money in time-proven mutual funds.

The best chance for the average investor is to put money in an index fund.

—Bernie Madoff

Bernie Madoff is infamous as the mastermind behind the largest Ponzi scheme in world history. His risky and unsuccessful trading strategies and his efforts to cover them up with falsified trading records that showed high, steady, risk-free returns lured in sixty-five billion dollars in investments from some of the smartest, most sophisticated investors in the world. And yet, when he actually took a moment to give personal finance advice after his fall from grace, he provided wisdom that everyone should follow: low-cost index mutual funds are the best option for most investors, and, if more financial advisors and journalists told people that, Americans' retirement portfolios would be a lot healthier.

Indeed, if Bernie Madoff somehow becomes the one to convince people to pursue simple, low-cost investment strategies like buying and holding index funds, he will have done far more good than evil in his time on earth.

Leaders must have a strong sense of renewal—an eagerness to create new opportunities through an entrepreneurial approach.

—Kay R. Whitmore,
Kodak president, in a 1986 address
to the Sloan School of Management at MIT

Whitmore took over as CEO of Kodak in 1990—and far from embracing a sense of renewal, he embodied a level of complacency that bordered on caricature; during a meeting with Bill Gates, presumably about ways to renew the company as it was losing market share to Polaroid, Mr. Whitmore fell asleep.

"They didn't believe the American public would buy another film," Alecia Swasy wrote in *Changing Focus: Kodak and the Battle to Save a Great American Company*, explaining the company's blasé attitude about competition.

Whitmore was pushed out of the company in 1993 and devoted much of the rest of his life to a new kind of renewal—Mormon missionary work. In 2012, Eastman Kodak filed for Chapter 11 bankruptcy protection. *Business Insider* named Whitmore one of the 15 Worst CEOs in American History.

There can be no question our country is in the worst economic crisis of our lifetimes. I also think there can be no question that it falls on us, the individuals, to find a way out of our own personal crisis.

—Curt Schilling

As a two-time World Series hero for the Boston Red Sox, Curt Schilling was one of the few Massachusetts residents who could provide a high-profile voice for conservative causes. On talk radio and on Twitter, he spoke out for the Republican platform: personal responsibility, limited government intervention in markets, and low taxes. He introduced John McCain at events during the 2008 presidential campaign and taped a TV commercial for the senator.

But when this athlete turned gaming nerd decided he wanted to start his own video game company, he abandoned his ruggedly individualistic values. Passed over by venture capitalists and rapidly draining his own nine-figure baseball fortune, Schilling turned to the state of Rhode Island for help. Desperate for job creation in 2010, the state guaranteed seventy-five million dollars in bonds to help finance the growth of his company, 38 Studios. Two years later, the company was on the ropes, and Schilling was begging for additional state assistance. The state declined, 38 Studios went bankrupt, the cash-strapped state was left on the hook for the debt, and Schilling's personal fortune was gone. He was forced to sell the bloody sock he wore during the 2004 World Series to pay off his creditors.

Schilling later blamed the state of Rhode Island and Governor Lincoln Chafee for not providing him with enough taxpayer money.

The no-money-down subprime loan
is the most dangerous product in
existence and there can be nothing
more toxic.

—Angelo Mozilo, then CEO of
Countrywide Financial, in a 2006 e-mail

The story of Angelo Mozilo, a butcher's son who rose to become the titan of the mortgage industry before collapsing into infamy as a poster child for everything that was wrong with the housing market of the 2000s, is a sad one.

Mozilo's internal e-mails—introduced to the public when the SEC sued him for securities fraud—show a man who, better than perhaps anyone, saw the problems that aggressive financing would bring. In the beginning, his company, Countrywide, eschewed the irresponsible underwriting that its scrappier counterparts were basking in. In 2005, *Barron's* listed him as one of the thirty most-respected CEOs in America. But ultimately, shareholder demands and his thirst for market share led him to abandon his underwriting standards, and Countrywide was responsible for billions of dollars in foreclosures on loans that, as Mozilo had noted eloquently, never should have been made in the first place.

Still, Mozilo made and kept hundreds of millions of dollars from stock sales at the height of the housing bubble. To settle the SEC's fraud charges, he paid $67.5 million in fines (Countrywide paid twenty million dollars of that per the terms of his employment agreement) and agreed to a lifetime ban from serving as an officer or director of a public company—not that anyone was asking him to.

Discipline yourself, as I do, to always play the percentages, thereby creating that competitive edge that is integral to success. Furthermore, recognize, acknowledge, and accept when the percentages are not in your favor, so that you do not take on unnecessary risk.

—Lenny Dykstra in a column for TheStreet.com

With the help of CNBC's resident screamer Jim Cramer, former Major League Baseball All-Star Lenny "Nails" Dykstra became a media sensation for his financial brilliance. He had a contract for a never-to-be-published book whose working titles included *From Nails to Riches: How a Tobacco-Chewin' Baseball Hero Made Himself a Superstar in the World of Money* and *Nailing It Every Time: Ten Rules for Following Lenny Dykstra's Stock Market Success*. He was also working on developing a new reality TV show called *Til Debt Do Us Part*, in which the former slugger would counsel couples on their finances. His magazine, *The Players Club*, was Dykstra's vision for "players helping players" to ensure that their fortunes would last a lifetime.

Unfortunately, Nails couldn't nail the discipline he so lauded. In 2007, he bought Wayne Gretzky's house with virtually nothing down for $18.5 million. He quickly lost it to foreclosure, and his magazine empire folded after Dykstra ran out of money to pay his employees. Dykstra's former photo editor wrote a blistering profile for *GQ* titled "You Think Your Job Sucks? Try Working for Lenny Dykstra."

Dykstra landed in bankruptcy, and then served time in prison for grand theft auto and filing a false financial statement—part of a crime spree that also reportedly included showing his penis to women he found on the Craigslist jobs page.

As Dykstra once described his earnings from baseball in an HBO interview: "Pay your agent, pay taxes, take care of your family, buy the nice house and now you got your dick in your hand, basically." He emerged from prison in mid-2013, and, desperate for cash, he's now making the rounds at autograph shows. For twenty-five dollars, he'll sign *anything*—a smart, low-risk financial strategy.

Focus on uncertainty first and
then think about returns second.

—Myron Scholes in a 2010 speech at the
University of Maryland Smith School of Business

Myron Scholes is that special kind of hypocrite: a Nobel laureate academic with an expertise in risk management and derivatives valuation who, when he decided to actually go into the field as a hedge fund manager, was partly responsible for the largest hedge fund collapse in world history. Beginning with a billion dollars in capital—lured in by Scholes' Nobel pedigree—Long-Term Capital Management posted good returns in the short run. But following the 1997 Asian financial crisis and the 1998 Russian financial crisis, the fund—which was borrowing $250 for every dollar its investors put up—lost $4.6 billion in less than four months and was subsequently bailed out under the supervision of the Federal Reserve.

But the fun wasn't over yet: the IRS disallowed one hundred million dollars in losses claimed by the fund on the grounds that it had set up sham transactions to generate tax benefits—and singled out Scholes as one of the people responsible for the scheme. Scholes testified that he was "not an expert with regard to taxes"—an assertion complicated by the fact that he had coauthored a $130 textbook called *Taxes and Business Strategy*.

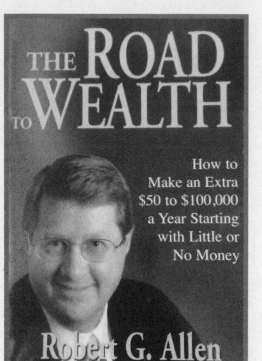

THE ROAD TO WEALTH

How to Make an Extra $50 to $100,000 a Year Starting with Little or No Money

Robert G. Allen

Assisted by Thomas R. Painter

How many millionaires do you know who have become wealthy by investing in savings accounts? I rest my case.

—Robert G. Allen, *Creating Wealth: Retire in Ten Years Using Allen's Seven Principles of Wealth*

How many get-rich-quick gurus do you know who went broke and then filed for Chapter 7 bankruptcy? Now you know one. In 1986, Allen, whose book *Nothing Down: A Proven Program That Shows You How to Buy Real Estate with Little or No Money Down* was at one time the bestselling real estate guide of all time, lost everything; he claimed the bankruptcy was caused by an avalanche that destroyed his house, but he also had huge amounts of tax liens and debts to Neiman Marcus, Citibank Visa, and the publishers of his books on how to get rich.

But ya can't keep a good—or at least shameless—man down. Allen didn't let his bankruptcy stop him: in 1987, he published *The Road to Wealth: How to Create Lifetime Streams of Cash Flow*, and since then he's authored or co-authored at least ten other wealth-building books, many of which have been bestsellers with a combination of obvious but good advice and dangerous advice.

Perhaps he'd be better off writing a cautionary tale. As real estate writer John T. Reed, whose website keeps tabs on the legal foibles of America's most prominent real estate "experts," puts it: "I think Allen has an interesting story to tell. But it's not the one he sells. He should speak about real estate investment the way a reformed alcoholic speaks about drinking." And if he went on a tour doing that, and put all of the money in a savings account, he'd probably be able to get and stay rich. That's not generally the optimal investment strategy, but for a guy with Allen's track record, it's probably the best choice.

Greed is not good. . . . Every deal
is a series of negotiations, and
negotiation is not about
taking or winning; it's more often
about sharing and compromise.

—Lou Pearlman,
*Bands, Brands, & Billions: My Top 10
Rules for Making Any Business Go Platinum*

In the mid- to late-1990s, the corpulent Lou Pearlman was the king of the boy bands, having created the Backstreet Boys, *NSYNC, O-Town, and LFO. The contracts he'd signed with the young performers generated controversy and lawsuits, but his ear and eye for what would sell were unquestionable.

But in 2006, Pearlman was exposed as having run one of the largest and longest-running Ponzi schemes in U.S. history, leaving investors in the lurch for $447 million; he'd forged documents, inflated financials, and induced banks into investing in companies that didn't exist.

Pearlman's fall is a classic case of the perils of excessive greed; unlike nearly every other Ponzi schemer, Pearlman had an enormously profitable cash-flow generating business—made more profitable by the fact that, according to lawsuits filed by every band he'd represented other than US5, Pearlman ripped off his clients. He fled to Indonesia but was eventually apprehended and sentenced to twenty-five years in prison with an unusual carve-out: his sentence would be reduced by one month for every million dollars he helped the bankruptcy trustee recover. While he's been languishing in jail, his 16,500-square-foot home has been sold at auction, along with keepsakes like a Daffy Duck figurine (fifty dollars), a bookcase (ten dollars), and a life-size Yoda statue.

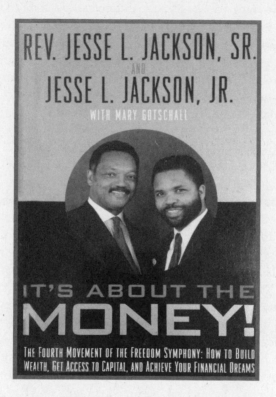

Living above your means is
financial sin.

—Jesse Jackson Jr., *It's About the Money!: The
Fourth Movement of the Freedom Symphony:
How to Build Wealth, Get Access to Capital,
and Achieve Your Financial Dreams*

Jesse Jackson Jr. rode his father's coattails to a personal finance guide published by Random House, along with a seat in the United States House of Representatives.

After resigning from Congress in 2012, citing bipolar disorder and gastrointestinal issues, Jackson pled guilty to one count of mail and wire fraud; it seems that Jackson used $750,000 in campaign money on personal expenses—including a fedora worn by Michael Jackson, elk heads, cashmere capes, and a guitar signed by Eddie Van Halen. In August 2013, he was sentenced to thirty months in prison, where he most certainly will not be living above his means.

Put together an open mind with a desire to succeed and you have the basic ingredients for starting a business, no matter how young you are.

—Barry Minkow, *Making it in America*

At age eighteen, Barry Minkow became the youngest CEO of a publicly traded company in U.S. history when his ZZZZ Best carpet cleaning company began trading on the NASDAQ. His story of entrepreneurial bootstrapping was perfect for the Reagan era, and he appeared on *Oprah* and wrote a self-help memoir; then he went to prison when the whole thing turned out to be a Ponzi scheme. While incarcerated, he found Jesus—who spends a ton of time in prisons, apparently—became an evangelical pastor and wrote a *New York Times* bestseller about his recovery from white-collar crime and the more than a billion dollars in fraud he'd helped regulators uncover. Then he went back to prison again for securities fraud—a round-trip from inspirational icon to convicted felon to inspirational icon to convicted felon. He's currently serving a five-year sentence.

PART TWO

INTEGRITY!

For most of us, the idea of having to be told to live with integrity seems absurd. If you actually have to be told not to lie, aren't you hopeless?

Probably. And as these cases illustrate, if you're inclined to advise others about the importance of being earnest . . . you are likely to end up in prison.

Promise only what you can deliver, and deliver what you promise.

—Charles J. Givens, *Super Self: Doubling Your Personal Effectiveness*

In the 1980s, Charles J. Givens was among the most successful personal finance gurus on the planet; he had a million-copy bestseller and as Bryant Gumbel once put it on the *Today* show, "When Charles Givens talks, everyone listens."

More sober critics had a different view; *Forbes* magazine called one of Givens's books "a useless, misleading, error-filled heap of bunkum," even as Simon & Schuster handed him a three-book, three-million-dollar contract. "I always dreamed of being able to write a best-selling book. This was a kid who couldn't spell. One of the things I learned is that you don't need to know a whole lot of spelling to write a best-seller," he once told *People* magazine.

The problem for Givens—besides being barely literate— was that ultimately, he couldn't deliver what he promised. The state of Florida sued him in 1993 for fraud, and in 1996, a California jury ruled that Givens had ripped off twenty-nine thousand of his how-to-get-rich customers, who were quickly handed a judgment of fourteen million dollars. Among the problems? Givens had misrepresented his past successes and the success of his past students, failed to comply with his refund policy, and just generally overhyped his worthless products.

"Givens lied about his past," a lawyer for the plaintiffs told *The New York Times*. "The way he made his money was not by using the strategies he sold but rather by selling the strategies themselves."

Givens died of cancer in 1998, still embroiled in litigation and investigations from all fronts, and it took four years for the fighting over his estate to conclude. It wasn't pretty: Givens, who had made millions with books like *Wealth Without Risk: How to Develop a Personal Fortune Without Going Out on a Limb*, died with assets of $2.8 million against debts of eighty-six million dollars—reflecting an inability to deliver what he'd promised. His family was left with nothing, and his wife, who was twenty years his junior and hadn't worked in years, began looking for jobs as a schoolteacher.

You will be confronted with questions every day that test your morals. Think carefully, and for your sake do the right thing, not the easy thing.

—Dennis Kozlowski in a 2002 commencement speech at Saint Anselm College

Around the turn of the millennium, former Tyco CEO Dennis Kozlowski became, along with Ken Lay of Enron and Bernie Ebbers of WorldCom, a universal symbol of the malfeasance, self-dealing, greed, and testosterone-gone-wild nature of corporate America—and his fall began with a tax evasion charge that forced his resignation less than three weeks after that speech .

As the CEO of Tyco, he was known as "Deal a Day Dennis"—and frequent acquisitions were a cornerstone of the strategy that led to consistent growth in Tyco's revenues, earnings, and stock price. But regulators argued—and the company eventually admitted—that the acquisitions had been used to artificially inflate Tyco's earnings.

Then there was the matter of Kozlowski's pay, which, a jury eventually concluded—with the help of a home video of his birthday party featuring togas and statues of *David* shooting vodka from their penises—had been bolstered by more than fifty million dollars in unauthorized bonuses. He vehemently denied any wrongdoing, telling *60 Minutes* in an in-prison interview that the jury had convicted him because of his wealth.

When he was facing the parole board, he changed his tune. "I knew I was doing something wrong at some level when I did it. My conscience told me one thing, but my sense of entitlement allowed me to rationalize what I did," he explained. "After I was in prison for a bit and thinking hard about what I did, I recognized my rationalizations were just that." That helped to secure his release from prison, and he now works as a clerk at a software company.

Truth is easier to remember than fiction. The reason that lie detectors work is that the act of lying creates a physical reaction in your body: your pulse quickens, your blood pressure increases, and often you begin to sweat—all signs of stress. Clearly your body does not think that lying is good, so imagine what it might be doing to your soul. It is important not only to speak the truth but also to stand up for the truth when others are wrong.

—Newt Gingrich, *5 Principles for a Successful Life: From Our Family to Yours*

Gingrich, in a testament to his lack of shame, provided his integrity advice in a book published more than a decade *after* the scandals that led to his downfall from his role as Speaker of the House—and a few years before his improbable rise as, ever-so-briefly, a legitimate contender for the 2012 GOP presidential nomination. Two affairs had led to two divorces—one of which was ongoing as he ripped President Clinton for his marital infidelities—and a House ethics investigation had undermined his tenure as Speaker. During the 2012 campaign, allegations about his ties to the mortgage industry dogged him. When he denied any lobbying experience, Congressman Barney Frank called him "a lobbyist and a liar."

In an interview with CBN, Gingrich explained his past infidelities with a pitch-perfect humblebrag: "There's no question at times in my life, partially driven by how passionately I felt about this country, that I worked far too hard and things happened in my life that were not appropriate."

The day you take complete responsibility for yourself, the day you stop making any excuse, that's the day you start to the top.

—O. J. Simpson in a 1975 *Playboy* interview

Mr. Simpson's definition of taking complete responsibility was different from most after the 1994 double homicide of his ex-wife and her friend. After an acquittal that stunned America and more than a decade of denials, he decided in 2006 to come clean about the murders—sort of. O.J.'s plan was to hedge on whether he was the murderer with a television special called *O. J. Simpson: If I Did It, Here's How It Happened* and a for-profit memoir called *If I Did It.*

When prepublication outrage exploded, the book was canceled, and by 2007, O. J. Simpson was back in jail following an arrest for armed robbery and kidnapping; he's currently serving a thirty-three-year sentence, but there is still hope! In late 2012, a judge agreed to reopen the case and explore Simpson's contention that incompetent representation entitled him to a new trial in the armed robbery case.

We must transform our government so that it is as ethical and wise as all of New York.

—Eliot Spitzer in his January 1, 2007, gubernatorial inaugural address

First as New York's attorney general and then as its governor, Eliot Spitzer built a national reputation as a media-savvy crusader for ethics in business and in government; he was among the biggest foes of corruption on Wall Street. Then his career came crashing down when it turned out that he was a client of Emperors Club VIP, where he paid as much as $3,100 per hour for prostitutes.

Post-fall, Spitzer—with a supporting wife and a huge amount of family money—might have taken some time off for self-examination and perhaps devoted his energy to public interest legal work. Instead, lacking the capacity for any sense of self outside of his public life, the narcissist landed gigs on nearly every cable news network, but he failed to draw an audience. Next, he ran for New York City Comptroller in the 2013 Democratic primary. He lost.

Winning is about heart. . . . It's got to be in the right place.

—Lance Armstrong

Few people inspired Americans more than Lance Armstrong; after beating testicular cancer, he came back to win a record seven consecutive Tour de France competitions between 1999 and 2005.

And all he needed was hard work, a positive attitude, steroids, blood transfusions, and terrifying threats leveled at anyone who might expose him.

He eventually confessed to using performance-enhancing drugs in every one of his Tour de France wins in a 2013 interview with Oprah Winfrey years after everyone else knew he was guilty beyond any doubt. He admitted to having been a "bully" and "a guy who expected to get whatever he wanted and to control every outcome." But with that confession came a lawsuit from the United States Postal Service demanding the return of all the endorsement money it had paid him. Virtually all his other endorsement deals have disappeared. And with Armstrong's earning power permanently impaired, it could spell his financial ruin—on top of his already ruined reputation.

No matter what your dreams and goals, you can never go wrong if you give them all you've got.

—Alex Rodriguez, *Out of the Ballpark*

At one time, Alex Rodriguez was enough of a role model to have his own children's book published by Harper-Collins: *Out of the Ballpark*. He was a baseball prodigy and well on his way to a Hall of Fame career when he left the Seattle Mariners to sign a record contract with the Texas Rangers in 2000. After years of denials of performance-enhancing drug use, he admitted in 2009 to having used steroids while with the Rangers—driven, he said, by the enormous pressure that came with the size of the contract. But, he said, he hadn't used illegal drugs since.

Then he was embroiled in the second performance-enhancing drugs scandal of his career—suggesting, if Major League Baseball's allegations were to be believed, that for A-Rod, his dreams and goals required all he had and some stuff drug dealers had, too. While all the other players caught in the 2013 scandal accepted their penalties, Rodriguez appealed the suspension and then sued Major League Baseball over what he alleged was a vast conspiracy to keep him out of the game, without ever really saying that he hadn't used the drugs he was accused of using. Assuming he never plays again in the majors, he'll finish his career fifth on the all-time list for home runs—and with one of the worst reputations of anyone in the history of sports who isn't named Jerry Sandusky or O. J. Simpson.

I think the challenge is you have
to say "Suspend your disbelief."

—Beverly Hall, *Voices for Democracy: Struggles
and Celebrations of Transformational Leaders*

In an American public school system plagued by under-achievement and high dropout rates, few leaders inspired optimism quite like Atlanta Public Schools superintendent Beverly Hall. In 2009, she was named Superintendent of the Year, and in 2010, President Obama nominated her to the National Board for Education Sciences. She'd rubbed elbows with Bill Gates, offered advice on educational re-form to Michael Bloomberg, and collected more than four hundred thousand dollars per year for her efforts—largely because of performance bonuses tied to standardized test scores that rose higher each year as disadvantaged urban youth others had given up on proved that they could suc-ceed in school.

But like most inspirational success stories that teach us to believe in ourselves and one another, this one was a total scam—observers had heeded Hall's call to suspend their disbelief, and children suffered as a result. A massive amount of cheating was discovered and questions about whether top administrators had been involved circulated. In March 2013, Dr. Hall and thirty-four others were indicted on charges that they had executed a systematic plan to falsify test results and enrich themselves with ill-gotten bonuses. Hall was charged with racketeering, theft, influencing wit-nesses, conspiracy, and making false statements, and she faces up to forty-five years in prison if convicted.

In the wake of Hall's retirement and eventual indict-ment, the district's new superintendent had to create reme-dial courses to help thousands of students whose falsified scores had landed them in classes they weren't qualified for. Meanwhile, federal grants to help struggling schools disappeared as a result of the fraudulently inflated performance. Hall is currently awaiting trial and has pled not guilty and denied knowledge of the cheating.

I think the most important thing is [to] restore a sense of idealism and end the cynicism in state government. Bring to the job a desire to really make things happen and help people and give confidence back to the public.

—Rod Blagojevich, 2002

When Rod Blagojevich ascended to the Illinois governor's mansion in 2003, he did it with an image as a reformer—an honest, ethical guy who would clean up a state that had a decades-old reputation around the country for political corruption.

Instead, Blagojevich ended up operating in the grand tradition of Illinois politics. When then senator Barack Obama was elected president, Blagojevich essentially tried to auction off the Senate seat he was charged with filling—providing a wiretapped quote more memorable than his 2002 call for idealism: "I've got this thing and it's fucking golden. And I'm just not giving it up for fucking nothing."

Blagojevich became the fourth of Illinois's last seven governors to land in prison, and the cynicism continues with good reason.

PART THREE

THE COMPLETE IDIOT'S GUIDE TO
LEADERSHIP

Leadership is hard work, and it's intimidating to most people—and that's why the people who are attracted to the idea of being leaders are often interesting folks. In his book *The Wisdom of Psychopaths*, University of Oxford research psychologist Kevin Dutton provides a list of the top-ten careers paths for sociopaths; he includes CEOs, police, clergymen, and politicians.

As George Carlin once put it: "Leadership camp? Isn't that where Hitler went?"

When you know what you
are talking about, others will
follow you, because it's safe to
follow you.

—Richard Fuld's 2006 commencement
speech at University of Colorado Boulder

When Lehman Brothers CEO Richard Fuld gave this speech, he was at the height of his power—his visit to his alma mater was something of a triumphant homecoming, and a year later his company's stock price would hit an all-time high.

Less than two and a half years after that speech, Lehman Brothers was bankrupt—primarily because the company's employees, investors, and lenders had followed Fuld into dicey mortgages because they trusted that he knew what he was talking about. It was the largest bankruptcy in U.S. history and instantly transformed Fuld into a perennial top-five contender on worst CEO lists. He's buried under a barrage of lawsuits and has been quietly attempting to rebuild a career working for smaller firms.

If you are given a chance to be a role model, I think you should always take it because you can influence a person's life in a positive light, and that's what I want to do. That's what it's all about.

—Tiger Woods, 1997

Back in 1997—when Tiger Woods gave that line to *BusinessWeek*—he was at the early stages of a golf career that would make him a legend and a cult of personality that would earn him far more money off the course than he ever earned playing. His father produced two books on parenting based on his experiences with Tiger, and his wholesome image sold everything from golf clubs to Buicks.

In 2010, he lost twenty-two million dollars in endorsements after a bizarre string of scandals led to his divorce and his exposure as a pill-popping philanderer with a thing for Hooters waitresses.

He rekindled controversy in 2013 when, after winning a tournament, Nike ran an ad that quoted him saying "Winning takes care of everything"—a far cry from the would-be role model of his youth.

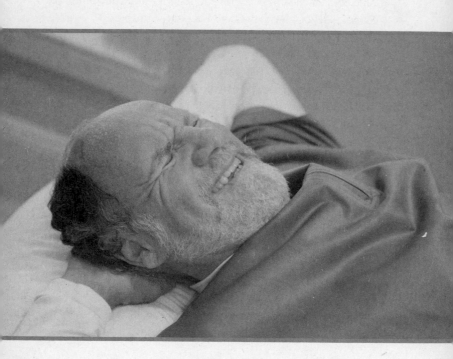

Taking a problem head on is better than hiding from it, even when it hurts. Not doing the right thing because it's too hard or too uncomfortable is not acceptable. Not today, and not ever.

—Jon Corzine

Jon Corzine was a former Goldman Sachs CEO who, after a 1999 battle with future Treasury secretary Henry Paulson cost him his kingdom, went on to serve as governor of New Jersey from 2006 to 2010. After losing his reelection bid to Chris Christie, Corzine took over as CEO of MF Global—and in 2011, after a series of futures bets made at Corzine's behest soured, he led the company to a spot on the list of the ten largest bankruptcies in U.S. history.

But the company didn't deal with its insolvency head on. Rather, it dipped into customer funds to pay off creditors. The customers didn't think it was the right thing, and they didn't think it was acceptable.

In April 2013, the company's bankruptcy trustee sued Corzine, accusing him of leading the company on a risky path of doom. The case is pending.

Man is the only creative animal
on earth, though paradoxically
his resistance to change
sometimes can be almost
heroically obstinate.

—Robert S. McNamara, *The Essence
of Security: Reflections in Office*

Robert S. McNamara had been president of Ford for less than five weeks when president-elect John F. Kennedy approached him about serving as Treasury secretary; he turned it down but quickly accepted a gig as secretary of defense. Almost immediately, he was a leading proponent of the strategy that led to the Cuban Missile Crisis.

But McNamara's real claim to fame was his manipulation of evidence to justify a war to Congress and the public. Later, McNamara became privately skeptical of the likelihood of success in the Vietnam War, but he persisted out of loyalty and his heroically obstinate resistance to change.

Later in life, McNamara was contrite: in a 1995 memoir, he noted that he had been "wrong, terribly wrong" about the Vietnam War. In 2003, he explained that "None of our allies supported us. Not Japan, not Germany, not Britain or France. If we can't persuade nations with comparable values of the merit of our cause, we'd better reexamine our reasoning."

Time magazine named him one of the ten worst cabinet members in U.S. history, noting that "Over the past two decades, McNamara has admitted lying to Congress about the justification for U.S. involvement in the war, and acknowledged that his errant judgment was partly responsible for [the loss of] nearly 60,000 American lives."

We choose hope over despair, possibilities over problems, optimism over cynicism. We choose to do what's right even when those around us say, "You can't do that."

—John Edwards's 2004 speech at the Democratic National Convention

John Edwards rose from poverty to build a career as a wildly successful ambulance-chasing attorney and then parlayed the same sleazy charisma that had helped him win over juries into a political career that culminated with a presidential bid during the 2008 election.

The small-town-family-man image came crumbling down when it was revealed, initially by the *National Enquirer* in 2007, that he had fathered a child with Rielle Hunter, a campaign worker, while his wife was battling cancer. A sex tape surfaced, followed by another campaign worker who, to cover for Edwards, claimed to have been the father. Edwards was eventually indicted, tried, and found not guilty on charges that he'd misused campaign funds to cover up the affair.

Publicly, he blamed his abandonment of his faith and ethics on that most twenty-first century of maladies: self-love. "In the course of several campaigns," he said, "I started to believe that I was special and became increasingly egocentric and narcissistic."

These days, Edwards lives in something resembling seclusion with no apparent future in public life. But he isn't ruling it out: "I don't think God's through with me," he said in 2012. "I really believe he thinks there's still some good things I can do." It seems likely that the public will choose hope and possibilities over Edwards's despair and problems.

Our motto is teamwork over talent.

—Mike Rice, Rutgers basketball coach

When Mike Rice took over as head coach of the Rutgers men's basketball program in 2010, he came with big expectations; the *Yahoo! Sports* headline declared "Rice is right at Rutgers." But over his first few seasons, he failed to turn around the team's losing record.

Then—as begin so many scandals these days—a video surfaced showing Rice hurling homophobic slurs at players, heaving balls at their heads, kicking them, and grabbing them by their shirts. It was so bad and so widely circulated that it was parodied on *Saturday Night Live*. Rice had previously been fined and suspended by the team, but when a disgruntled former employee leaked the video to the media, the school saw Rice's fund-raising and ticket-selling abilities permanently impaired—and fired him.

It's hard to imagine where Rice's next coaching job will come from, but if you're interested in helping him get back on his feet, you can always buy a copy of *All Access Rutgers Basketball Practice with Mike Rice*—a three-DVD, 441-minute, $149.99 extravaganza coproduced by Rice himself that promises to help you "learn a chaotic style of offensive and defensive play that will force your opponents to play outside of their comfort zone." As of 2013, Rice is still reportedly coaching his daughter's seventh grade team—as loudly and aggressively as ever, according to media reports.

"Selflessness" is the greatest asset an individual can have in a time of crisis. . . . The very fact that the crisis is bigger than the man himself takes his mind off his own problems. The natural symptoms of stress in a period of crisis do not become self-destructive as a result of his worry about himself but, on the other hand, become positive forces for creative action.

—Richard Nixon, *Six Crises*

In 1962, John F. Kennedy was riding high on the success of his book *Profiles in Courage*, and California gubernatorial candidate Richard Nixon decided he wanted a piece of his publishing success. So he published *Six Crises*, an instant bestseller that described six crises he'd faced in his career—and how he'd overcome them and what he'd learned from them.

In later years, the joke was that the book should have been published in loose-leaf so that readers could add updates on each new crisis. Nevertheless: Nixon preached the notion that, when directed at problems larger than an individual, stress could be a catalyst for accomplishment rather than self-destructiveness.

As president, Nixon's inability to focus on issues larger than himself led to his downfall—and his paranoia about perceived enemies led to self-destructive conduct that forced his resignation and undermined a career and legacy that had been otherwise successful on many of the more selfless issues Nixon confronted: environmental destruction, civil rights, and Sino-American relations.

PART FOUR

TIME WELL SPENT AND
A LIFE WELL LIVED

The most ethical hypocrites have the decency to claim a niche—and then lie about having special insight about it. Some will tell you what to do with money, some know how to save your relationships, and others can help you figure out what God wants.

This part is devoted to the special ones who have advice on *everything* about your life: how to spend your time, what to think, which things you should and shouldn't put in your body, and how to be imaginative. The people who are inclined to give such general advice are often the ones least worthy of the soapbox on which they stand. Still: it's good advice.

Think on the blessings of food
that you were able to eat today
when, not so many miles away,
people are starving to death. And
as you think on your abundance,
it'll cause you to think more about
doing something about those that
don't have.

—Jim Jones

Before Jim Jones gained international infamy as the leader of the largest mass-suicide in modern history, he was a San Francisco celebrity known for his church's racial inclusion, progressive politics, and emphasis on helping the poor. But there were also rumors and local media reports of paranoia, cultlike control, and physical abuse of his flock. When he moved his congregation to Guyana to set up a modestly titled socialist paradise called Jonestown, Jones's drug addiction and mental illness intensified. With concerned relatives pressuring the U.S. government to investigate Jones's activities, Congressman Leo Ryan traveled to Jonestown to check on the well-being of the people—and to make sure that they weren't being held against their will. After Congressman Ryan, an NBC cameraman, and several Jonestown residents who had asked to leave the cult were assassinated by Jones's security at the airstrip, Jones ordered all of the residents of Jonestown to drink cyanide-laced Flavor Aid. More than nine hundred people, including Jones, died in the mass murder-suicide, and "Drink the Kool-Aid" has entered the lexicon as a description of anyone who blindly follows a charismatic leader's orders.

Fear is the enemy, love is the cure. . . . Ask yourself: What is the most loving, caring thing I can do in this situation for all concerned? Then do it without judging the answer.

—Jeff Locker, *Teachings for a New World*

Jeff Locker was a successful motivational speaker in the 1990s; he had a consulting business and a book that promised to deliver better performance and better relationships through higher self-esteem. But by 2009, Locker's fortunes had taken a turn. He was deeply in debt—a judge had ordered him to return money he'd made investing in Lou Pearlman's Ponzi scheme (see page 38)—when he called his wife to tell her he had a flat tire and would be home late. He was then found stabbed to death in his car in Harlem. Police quickly apprehended Kenneth Minor, a homeless man, who was using Locker's debit card.

It all seemed like a tragic robbery gone bad, but when detectives arrived at Locker's home to tell his family, they didn't seem especially shocked. "I'm going back to bed," his daughter announced. Police eventually found instructions Locker had sent his wife about the fourteen million dollars in life insurance he'd recently purchased. The homeless suspect explained that Locker had given him his debit card in exchange for murdering him: suicide by hit man as a means of getting around his life insurance policy's clauses that barred payouts in the case of suicide. It was, Locker had apparently decided, the most loving thing he could do for his family.

The facts of the case were not in dispute: both the prosecution and the defense agreed that the hit man had simply held the knife while Locker lunged into it. But the jury, under the weight of the judge's instructions, didn't buy the defense: he was convicted of murder and sentenced to at least twenty years in prison, although he was recently granted a new trial. Meanwhile, Locker's life insurers denied coverage on the grounds that he'd lied on the applications.

In an interview with *48 Hours*, Minor seemed to express a certain sort of pride in the sordid act he'd participated in: "I just happened to be the building he jumped off of. . . . I was kind of privileged [that he chose me]. Nobody will ever see you again but me, and you chose me."

Our talk, the natural emission
of grandiosity within, kills our
momentum.

—Dick Morris, *The New Prince: Machiavelli
Updated for the Twenty-First Century*

Up until not all that long ago, few people had better reputations as political experts than Dick Morris. Whatever people thought of his character or lack of commitment to any particular ideological principles, the word for Dick Morris was *smart*. George Stephanopoulos later remembered that "Over the course of the first nine months of 1995, no single person had more power over the president." He was a contributor on Fox News and widely respected for his insight into the political process and, in particular, his expertise as a pollster, especially in conservative circles.

Then, in the months leading to the 2012 election—right up to Election Day—Morris made the biggest and most grandiose prediction of his career. In appearances on cable news shows, in his columns, and in YouTube videos, Morris predicted a landslide victory for Mitt Romney: 325 electoral votes to Obama's 213. He predicted that Romney would win every state McCain had won in 2008, plus Florida, Indiana, Virginia, North Carolina, Colorado, Iowa, Ohio, New Hampshire, Pennsylvania, Wisconsin, and Minnesota. He also predicted that Romney would win by five to ten percentage points in the popular vote.

By early evening on election night, Morris's considerable momentum as a political pundit was gone. Cartoonist Marshall Ramsey tweeted that "The Mayans, Dick Morris and the Groundhog should be put in prognosticator timeout." Blogger Andrew Sullivan named an annual award given for "stunningly wrong political, social and cultural predictions" after the fallen soothsayer, and Fox News promptly dumped him as a contributor. He landed a job as a local talk radio host for 1210 WPHT Philadelphia—a steep decline for a man once hailed as a political savant.

It is easier to get into something
than to get out of it.

—Donald Rumsfeld, 1974

Donald Rumsfeld was fond of circulating his own lists of folksy advice to his subordinates back when he was head of President Ford's transition team and later as a White House chief of staff.

Unfortunately, even the best-laid aphorisms couldn't save Rumsfeld from a string of legacy-ruining blunders during his service as President George W. Bush's secretary of defense. On February 7, 2003, Rumsfeld spoke to troops and explained that the conflict in Iraq they had just begun would not last long. "It is unknowable how long that conflict will last," he said. "It could last six days, six weeks. I doubt six months."

With Rumsfeld leading the charge, the entire Bush administration seemed to have been deluded about the cost and length of the war. For his efforts, *Time* magazine named Rumsfeld one of the ten worst cabinet members in U.S. history. The combat mission in Iraq didn't officially end until 2010.

When you focus only on today
you make poor decisions and end
up mortgaging tomorrow.

—Andy Pettitte, *Strike Zone: Targeting a
Life of Integrity & Purity*

In his 2005 abstinence-oriented self-help book for Christian teens, star pitcher Andy Pettitte addressed the importance of purity and hard work. He discussed his intense off-season training regimen with Roger Clemens and their trainer, "Brian"—who, we'd later learn, was Brian McNamee, the star witness in the government's perjury trial of Clemens, who had been accused of lying about his use of performance-enhancing drugs.

Clearly Pettitte learned a lot from these sessions because, as it turned out, he was also doping, having obtained prescriptions for human growth hormone for his father, who was suffering from a serious heart condition.

"Was it stupid? Yeah, it was stupid. Was I desperate? Yeah, I was probably desperate," he explained at a press conference after the drug use came to light. "I wish I never would have done it, obviously, but I don't consider myself a cheater, no."

Southern charm is real. It
works. . . . I want people to feel
good about bein' with me, and
bein' nice to them makes it
happen.

—Paula Deen, *It Ain't All About the Cookin'*

In her *New York Times* bestselling self-help memoir, wildly popular TV chef Paula Deen talked about Southern charm—why it works and how anyone, Southern or not, can develop it. She followed that up with a section called "Never Judge a Book by Its Cover."

But a deposition revealed that Deen's charm and open-mindedness doesn't necessarily extend to African Americans. She admitted to having used the *n* word in private conversations and seemed to hedge on whether the word was intrinsically offensive. She insisted she wasn't racist.

A former employee alleged in a lawsuit that Ms. Deen had mused on the possibilities for a wedding catered only by African Americans: "Well what I would really like is a bunch of little n****** to wear long-sleeve white shirts, black shorts and black bow ties, you know in the Shirley Temple days, they used to tap dance around" the lawsuit claims Deen said. "Now that would be a true southern wedding, wouldn't it? But we can't do that because the media would be on me about that."

That same lawsuit alleges that African American employees at Uncle Bubba's Oyster House, a restaurant operated by a company Ms. Deen owns half of, were required to use a separate entrance and separate bathrooms. "Contrary to media reports, Ms. Deen does not condone or find the use of racial epithets acceptable," Deen's attorney, William Franklin, told the Associated Press. The lawsuit was dismissed with prejudice, and the warring parties reconciled in statements released to the media. "Moving forward my team and I are working to review the workplace environment issues that were raised in this matter and to retool all of my businesses operations," Deen said in the statement.

Sometimes we need to let ourselves go, and sometimes we need to escape from what we know. There is a time for every kind of thinking.

—Jonah Lehrer, *Imagine: How Creativity Works*

In his early thirties, Jonah Lehrer was a wunderkind staff writer at *The New Yorker*, a blogger for Wired.com, and a frequent public radio commentator. His 2009 book *How We Decide*—published when Lehrer was just twenty-seven—was a mega-bestseller, gave him the platform to collect mid-five-figure checks for speaking engagements, and earned him praise as the best science writer to come along in a generation.

In 2012, his book *Imagine: How Creativity Works*, ruined his life when journalist Michael Moynihan exposed him as a fraud. Lehrer had gotten a bit too imaginative in his reporting and had fabricated quotes from Bob Dylan. He'd also plagiarized himself repeatedly, sold variations of the same articles to different outlets, gotten key details about the physiology of the brain wrong, taken scientific studies out of context, and misquoted people he'd interviewed. He was, in short, an unbelievably sloppy journalist who had manipulated data into neat, bite-size conclusions that played well on the lecture circuit. The time for Lehrer's kind of thinking, the public and the editors who'd made him a star decided, had passed.

After a firestorm of schadenfreude ensued, Lehrer resigned from his position as a staff writer at *The New Yorker*. In 2013, he scored a contract with Simon & Schuster to publish a book about love.

I never play it safe when I write a book. I bring myself to the edge of a cliff, trying something new. I'm not saying it hasn't been done before. I'm saying that I've never done it. To be safe is not to try. The challenge of trying something is what charges me up.

—Janet Dailey in a *Boston Globe* interview

From the late 1980s to the mid-1990s, there were few people who could touch Janet Dailey in the world of romance novels: her books sold at a rate of forty thousand copies per day in ninety countries, and she was pulling in more than a million dollars per year.

But in 1997, the extent to which Dailey was doing stuff she'd never done came to light when it was revealed that she'd plagiarized ideas and even verbatim text from fellow novelist Nora Roberts, who referred to the plagiarism, in decidedly unromantic terms, as "mind rape."

Her publisher pulled two of her books, and Dailey apologized publicly, though she fell short of actually taking responsibility, blaming her husband's medical issues and the death of the family dog for her transgressions.

And because this was the 1990s, she also cited an unspecified psychological disorder: "I recently learned that my essentially random and non-pervasive acts of copying are attributable to a psychological problem that I never even suspected I had," she said in a statement. "I have already begun treatment for the disorder and have been assured that, with treatment, this behavior can be prevented in the future." She has since returned to writing—and continues to score *New York Times* bestsellers.

When you let your imagination
win, there's no limit to what you
can accomplish.

—Ron Johnson in a 2012 speech at the Stanford
University School of Medicine

Ron Johnson built a sterling reputation as vice president of merchandising at Target before he left to run Apple's retail stores. During his seven and a half years at Apple, he earned four hundred million dollars and then left in November 2011 to serve as CEO of JCPenney, a failing retail chain desperate for new ideas.

He might have done better paying attention to Warren Buffett's words of wisdom: "When a management with a reputation for brilliance tackles a business with a reputation for bad economics, it is the reputation of the business that remains intact."

Upon Johnson taking over as CEO, JCPenney announced bold plans to revitalize its flagging stores. He got rid of coupons and unveiled a new store-within-a-store concept where each JCPenney would be turned into a mall within a mall with well-curated boutiques for each brand. He did no consumer testing—most likely inspired by his former boss Steve Jobs's hatred of focus groups—but promised he could, once again, revolutionize retailing. Meanwhile, he was criticized for a detached management style after opting to commute several days a week by private jet to the company's headquarters in Texas instead of permanently relocating from his home in California.

Sales plunged, the company chalked up a nine-digit loss in a single quarter, and Johnson was ousted after a year and a half on the job as analysts fretted that the losses born of an overactive imagination could be driving the company toward bankruptcy.

What appears to be homicide is essentially suicide. Disrespect is used as an excuse to become violent. Manhood is falsely equated with being able to beat someone down or pack a 9mm.

—Ernest C. Garlington, *Roots of a Man: 7 Principles for Growing Strong and Powerful*

D r. Ernest C. Garlington seemed to have it all: He was in his thirties with a beautiful family and his own three-acre retreat center where he provided therapy services and a life skills group for young men along with a men's empowerment group. He specialized in training young men from difficult urban backgrounds to overcome their environmental pressures and pursue lives of productivity and nonviolence with Christian values.

He was doing so well, apparently, that he had thirty thousand dollars to blow on a hitman.

Garlington was married to Darlene Powell-Garlington, who was recently divorced from Derek Hopson. Mr. Garlington took a strong disliking to Hopson, and so he paid a convicted felon thirty thousand dollars to kill him. The murder attempt was unsuccessful after Hopson dodged the first bullet and the gun jammed on the second attempt. A police surveillance tape of Garlington set up in the wake of the attacks captured him talking to another convicted felon about burning down the house of a lawyer he didn't like and shooting his stepdaughter's high school principal.

Garlington is currently serving thirty-three years at a maximum security prison in Connecticut. There is still an active online community of his supporters, who insist on his innocence. At his sentencing, the judge addressed them: "In my opinion, the evidence was overwhelming. For those of you that were here, you weren't listening or you had blinders on."

While we all need rest and relaxation, it becomes very easy for leisure to descend into slothfulness, laziness, and irresponsibility. . . . Exercise your mind and your body in responsible and fulfilling ways.

—William J. Bennett, *The Book of Man: Readings on the Path to Manhood*

As secretary of education under Ronald Reagan, William Bennett embodied the traditional law-and-order values of the administration: pro-religion in the classroom and pro—war on drugs.

Post-politics, Bennett carved out a career as a moralist commentator and author with tomes like *The Book of Man: Readings on the Path to Manhood* and *The Broken Hearth: Reversing the Moral Collapse of the American Family.* He scored a big hit in 1993 with *The Book of Virtues: A Treasury of Great Moral Stories*, which he followed up, predictably, with *The Children's Book of Virtues*.

So it was a bit of a shock when *Washington Monthly*, citing internal casino documents, reported in a 2003 story titled "The Bookie of Virtue" that this neo-Victorian had lost more than eight million dollars gambling over the past decade. "Relentless Moral Crusader Is Relentless Gambler" was the *New York Times* headline. Over one two-month period, Bennett had wired a casino $1.4 million to cover his losses. Bennett explained that he didn't gamble the "milk money" and could afford his seven-digit gambling losses—and at $50,000 per speech on how to be a responsible man, he's probably right.

"There's a term in the trade for this kind of gambler," a casino source who had seen Bennett play told *Washington Monthly.* "We call them losers."

There's nothing good about
drug use. We know it. It destroys
individuals. It destroys families.
Drug use destroys societies. Drug
use, some might say, is destroying
this country.

—Rush Limbaugh on *The Rush
Limbaugh Show*, October 5, 1995

Rush Limbaugh was a relentless moral crusader for tougher drug laws, and he showed little sympathy for people struggling with substance abuse. In 2003, he was investigated by the Palm Beach state attorney for illegally obtaining prescriptions for oxycodone and hydrocodone; he paid thirty thousand dollars in exchange for prosecutors dropping the charges, and he agreed to complete an eighteen-month therapy regimen. In 2006, airport officials confiscated Viagra from his luggage because it had not been prescribed to him.

If we wanted to go after him for his Bible-thumping family-values hypocrisy, we might note that he's been married four times. But in the interest of limiting this entry to his drug-abuse hypocrisy, we'll leave that out.

There is also a profound philosophical change taking place in this country—an emerging recognition of the role our individual consciousness plays in mediating our inner experience and our interaction with the environment.

—Dr. Michael Weiner, *The Complete Book of Homeopathy: A Comprehensive Manual of Natural Healing*

In the 1970s and 1980s, Dr. Michael Weiner built a following as an author of thoughtful, well-researched guides to alternative medicine. He combined homeopathic advice with a certain new age sensibility in books such as *Healing Children Naturally*.

Then he changed his name to Michael Savage, became a leading conservative talk radio host, and authored bestselling books such as *Liberalism Is a Mental Disorder* and *The Death of the White Male*. He built a reputation as one of the least individually conscious people on the planet with controversial comments about illegal immigrants, Muslims, gays (in response to one caller: "Oh, so you're one of those sodomites. . . . You should only get AIDS and die, you pig. How's that?"), and children with autism ("I'll tell you what autism is. In ninety-nine percent of the cases, it's a brat who hasn't been told to cut the act out."). In 2009, the United Kingdom barred him from entering the country on the grounds that he was "considered to be engaging in unacceptable behaviour by seeking to provoke others to serious criminal acts and fostering hatred which might lead to inter-community violence."

Direction is the key word here. Direction is what it takes to get you from where you are—to where you want to be. You have to remember, too, that direction can also take you from where you are—to where you really don't want to be, so your choice of direction is extremely critical.

—Gary Shawkey, *If I Can . . . Anybody Can . . .*

Gary Shawkey was a motivational speaker and Internet marketer; the back cover of his 2003 book notes that "His personal life reads more like a movie script and his business story offers promise and hope to those who feared they could never succeed."

In 2011, he stole $1.2 million from a retiree and then killed a prospective investor on a sailboat off the coast of Southern California. When questioned by investigators, Shawkey spun an elaborate tale of a sea urchin farm, pirates, and underwater fences. The jury laughed as they watched a recording of the interrogation and then sent him to prison for the rest of his life. No word yet on whether his cellmate will offer him his choice of direction.

You're not disabled by the disabilities you have, you are abled by the abilities you have.

—Oscar Pistorius

This Olympic champion with prosthetic legs wasn't going to let his disability stop him from shooting his girl-friend through a bathroom door. Score one for equality.

The shooting immediately cost Pistorius endorsement deals with Nike, Oakley, and Thierry Mugler—although while out on bail he was cleared to travel to participate in competitions. He is currently awaiting trial. Pistorius, who admits to having shot the woman through a bathroom door four times, says that he thought it was an intruder, but the prosecution isn't buying it. At press time, his trial for premeditated murder was set to begin in March 2014.

Life teaches you every day the reason to live is to love and protect loved ones who aren't capable of defending themselves.

—Derek Medina, *How I Saved Someone's Life and Marriage and Family Problems Thru Communication*

Derek Medina was hardly a self-help impresario, but he was trying; the 31-year-old, 6'2", 200-pound South Miami property manager thanked his wife Jennifer Alfonso in the acknowledgments of his self-published e-book *How I Saved Someone's Life and Marriage and Family Problems Thru Communication*.

Then Medina made headlines when he allegedly murdered his wife and posted gruesome pictures of her body on Facebook. He turned himself in to police and was charged with first-degree murder.

He is awaiting trial, and his other books currently available include captivating titles such as *If the World Ended Today How Would You React to Saving the World or Helping the World or Would it All be Over for You*, *World Just Ask Yourself Why We Are Living a Life Full of Lies and How I an Emotional Writer Made All of My Professional Dreams Come True Blocking Society's Teachings*, *Attention World Save Yourself*, and *Humans Who Are Gifted and Can See the Supernatural Spirit Ghost World We Live in Called Ghost Haunted Adventures*.

If you're defined by your possessions, you're not defined.

—Tim Blixseth

Montana timber billionaire Tim Blixseth might have preached a gospel of nonmaterialism—but in the end, his own profligate spending and a slew of lawsuits led to his financial decline. Blixseth was sort of a cliché of real estate bubble nouveau riche: tons of debt and a high-rolling lifestyle. He built what *The New York Times* called "the world's only private golf and ski resort" in Big Sky, Montana, and he traveled the world on a fleet of private jets, racking up debt and real estate.

In 2007, *The Wall Street Journal* ran a glowing piece on Blixseth's divorce: "A Billionaire Divorce—and Not a Lawyer in Sight." The piece explained how the purported billionaire and his wife, Edra, had divided their assets over a glass of wine and remained on good terms after their separation. But they wound up in court quickly, with Edra accusing him of handing her assets that were encumbered by debt, while keeping the cash and debt-free assets to himself. He denies that, but she isn't buying it. "I would rather feel the cold steel of a revolver in the roof of my mouth and pull the trigger than to ever think about living a day with that man again," she told *The New York Times*. By 2009, Mr. Blixseth's financial life had spiraled into further decline. Blixseth was pushed into involuntary bankruptcy in September 2012, and the onslaught of litigation continues.

A word about
steroids: Don't
use them. . . .
Only a fool
becomes drug
dependent.
Fools have
no chance to
become stars
in baseball
or, probably,
in any other
aspect of life.
Stay clean.

—Jose Canseco,
*Strength Training
for Baseball*

Jose Canseco was twenty-five years old at the beginning of the 1990 season—two seasons removed from becoming the first player in history to hit forty home runs and steal forty bases—and his combination of speed and power made him seem destined for a Hall of Fame–caliber career.

It didn't quite work out that way. Canseco played his last game in 2001 and came up short of five hundred homers—one of the better power hitters in an era defined by them but not quite in the top tier. It was his next act that made Canseco's contribution to baseball. His book *Juiced: Wild Times, Rampant 'Roids, Smash Hits, and How Baseball Got Big* is widely credited as the book that ignited awareness of the steroid era in Major League Baseball.

"I was known as the godfather of steroids in baseball," he wrote in the book. "I introduced steroids into the big leagues back in 1985, and taught other players how to use steroids and growth hormone." So five years before proclaiming in his book that only fools use steroids, Canseco was introducing his teammates to them. Got that?

Canseco might have used steroids to become a star in baseball, but they didn't help his performance off the field. He got his ass kicked in a celebrity boxing event and battled to a draw against Danny Bonaduce. A 2008 A&E documentary showed Canseco's efforts to kick his steroid addiction and combat his body's resultant inability to produce testosterone. That same year, he was sentenced to twelve months' probation for trying to smuggle a fertility drug across the Mexican border and lost his home to foreclosure. In spite of numerous publicity stunts and reality TV appearances, Canseco filed for bankruptcy in 2012. But you can still follow him on Twitter for more wisdom, like this tweet from April 14, 2012: "Titanic 100 years wOw. Global warming couldve saved titanic. Sad to say." He also attempted to crowd-source a pro bono attorney to help him get his chandeliers back after his landlord evicted him.

Without kindness the mighty
are ruthless. Without kindness
the emotionally stable are
emotionally cold and hard.
Without kindness the intelligent
become arrogant.

—Robert H. Schuller,
*Hours of Power: My Daily Book of
Motivation and Inspiration*

Beginning with his *Hour of Power* television show in 1970, televangelist Robert H. Schuller quickly rose to become one of the most popular religious leaders in America. "If you can dream it, you can do it" is one of his more famous lines, and Schuller preached the power of positive thinking—focusing on empowerment and wealth rather than sin.

But a decade before Victoria Osteen made it fashionable (see page 154), Pastor Schuller was having problems with flight attendants. On July 28, 1997, Schuller refused orders from two flight attendants to place the garment bag containing his minister's robe in the overhead bin. The ground supervisor boarded the plane and Schuller obeyed his orders—but the fun was just beginning. When Schuller was served a dessert of grapes and cheese, he "[went] nuts," according to one flight attendant. "I am allergic to cheese," he proclaimed. "I can't even see cheese." He demanded grapes without cheese—actually using the phrase "all the grapes on the plane"—and was told that the grapes came prepackaged with the cheese. The seventy-year-old pastor then followed the flight attendant to the galley and—in an act that few on board likely considered kind—began shaking the younger man's shoulders. He denied the allegations and, in a deal with kind federal prosecutors, the charges were dropped in exchange for an apology and a one-thousand-dollar fine.

I've never been a passive person.
I've always felt that, if you think
something should be changed,
it's your responsibility to actively
pursue that change.

—Bob Filner, former San Diego mayor

When California congressman and later San Diego mayor Bob Filner made those comments, he was reflecting on the volunteer work he'd done as a Freedom Rider, helping to integrate buses when he was a teenager.

Unfortunately, as an adult, Filner also applied that can-do spirit to his interactions with women. On October 15, 2013, Filner pleaded guilty to felony false imprisonment "by violence, fraud, menace and deceit" and two counts of misdemeanor battery. He'd already resigned as mayor because of the allegations, which began with his former communications director alleging that he'd demanded kisses, asked that she work without panties, and put her in a headlock.

Prior to pleading guilty, Filner lashed out at his accusers, evoking the evils of the injustices he'd once fought against. He compared the allegations against him to a lynch mob. "I think he wants to redeem his original legacy, which was a wonderful one, and put this behind him," his attorney told reporters.

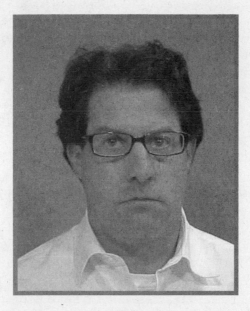

In wake of this Internet explosion, we must not forget to remain technologically responsible. To survive today's Internet e-mergency, we must navigate around the landmines. To survive tomorrow's Internet e-mergency, we must learn how to defuse them.

—Michael Fortino, *e-Mergency*

Michael Fortino was a successful motivational speaker and expert on time management. His dubious calculations on how much of their lives Americans spend engaged in mundane tasks (seven years in the bathroom, five years waiting in line, eight months opening junk mail) landed him mentions in *The New York Times*, *The Wall Street Journal*, *BusinessWeek*, and Harper's Index, and on the *Today* show, *The Tonight Show*, and *Good Morning America*.

President George H.W. Bush said that "Responsible Americans like Michael Fortino show concern for tomorrow's generation."

As it turned out, Fortino's concern for and interest in the younger generation was more than motivational: On November 4, 2005, during a speaking trip, Fortino was having trouble with his laptop. When he brought it to Best Buy for repairs, they discovered hundreds of images of child pornography and a browser history full of kiddie porn sites. Fortino had also rigged up a hidden camera in a small room on his boat and taped girls between the ages of eleven and sixteen changing clothes.

He eventually pleaded guilty and then landed in additional trouble when it turned out he'd forged letters to the United States Probation Service asking for leniency. He's currently serving twenty years in prison with no Internet access.

Reading is to the mind what food
is to the body.

—George W. Bush

Whatever your thoughts on President George W. Bush, one thing we should all be able to agree on is that he was not our most literate leader. He was famous for his malapropisms and reports that he preferred to have security briefings read to him, and when he was asked what his favorite books were as a child, he mentioned *The Very Hungry Caterpillar*—which was published when Bush was twenty-two years old.

For additional reading, check a crazy person's yard sale for a copy of *The Leadership Genius of George W. Bush: 10 Common Sense Lessons from the Commander in Chief*.

PART FIVE

RELATIONSHIPS: TILL DEATH (OR DOMESTIC VIOLENCE OR CRYSTAL METH AND GAY HOOKERS) DO US PART

Relationships are hard. The divorce rate in the United States is somewhere around 50 percent, and no amount of advice seems to be doing anything to budge that. In 2008, 13.5 million relationship books were sold—74 percent of those to women, who are more likely to blame themselves for failed relationships and see a need for self-improvement. Men, on the other hand, are more likely to just say "Screw it"—and if the relatively constant divorce rate is any indication of the efficacy of popular relationship advice, the guys may be on to something. So take some comfort in the fact that the people you or someone you know look to for relationship advice aren't so great at it either—and at least you (probably) didn't punch your wife in a hotel parking lot, set up a charity for the sole purpose of recruiting molestation victims, or tell the police that your enormous cache of child pornography was a healthy alternative to adult pornography.

I have always felt that forgiveness

is one of man's noblest virtues.

—Dear Abby

Sibling rivalry is normal but childhood animosities should diminish as people grow and mature. When this fails to occur, or worse yet, when the competitive spirit intensifies and bitter rivalry takes over, there is misery on both sides.

—Ann Landers

Not everyone knows it these days, but Ann Landers and Dear Abby were identical twin sisters: Esther Pauline Friedman and Pauline Esther Phillips, respectively. (What possessed their parents to name them both Pauline is the subject of another book.) With roughly one hundred million readers each, they have been the queens of advice from the mid-1950s on to the present, with their names carried on by new writers. And they seemed to have everything figured out—except how to have a civil relationship with each other.

The sisters were born in Iowa in 1918 and were close. They even had a double wedding ceremony on their twenty-first birthday. Just months after Esther became Ann Landers for the *Chicago Sun-Times*, her twin started the Dear Abby column. The competition for syndication led to a nasty sibling rivalry when Dear Abby was offered at a reduced rate to their hometown paper in exchange for that paper blacklisting Ann Landers. They didn't speak to each other for years, sort of reconciled, and then maintained a frosty relationship for the rest of their lives and careers.

Interestingly, the pair's daughters have also feuded publicly through the media.

God will bless your marriage to the degree to which you are obedient to his covenantal design. If you disobey the terms of the covenant, your marriage will fail. If you ignore the structures of your marriage relationship, you are vulnerable to disaster.

—Ted Haggard, *From This Day Forward: Making Your Vows Last a Lifetime*

Ted Haggard was a megachurch pastor and president of the thirty-million-member National Association of Evangelicals when disaster came. In an act that in most circles would be considered disobedience to the terms of the covenant, he used crystal meth while receiving happy endings from a gay prostitute he'd hired for massages.

When the prostitute went to the media—he later released a self-aggrandizing book about the episode called *I Had to Say Something: The Art of Ted Haggard's Fall*—Haggard's life came crashing down. He was banished from his church, stripped of his political power (he'd once had weekly conversations with Bush administration officials), and, as of 2009, was reduced to selling mortgage acceleration software door-to-door to try to make ends meet.

But like Jesus himself, Haggard staged a comeback: he now has a new—albeit smaller—church, and he also appeared on the reality show *Celebrity Wife Swap*. For one week, he swapped wives with Gary Busey, a tactic not specifically recommended in *From This Day Forward: Making Your Vows Last a Lifetime*.

But Haggard gets the last laugh; he and his wife are still together and—you knew this was coming, right?—in 2010 she released *Why I Stayed: The Choices I Made in My Darkest Hour*. Buoyed by a joint *Oprah* appearance—in which Haggard explained that his therapist told him he was "heterosexual with homosexual attachments"—it was a *New York Times* bestseller; *From This Day Forward* was not.

In the end, inappropriate sexual expressions (promiscuity, affairs, porn, prostitutes) are paths to avoid becoming a fully functional, adult human man.

—Dr. Laura Schlessinger, *Ten Stupid Things Men Do to Mess Up Their Lives*

Adult human Dr. Laura Schlessinger has built a career on being one of the nastiest, most judgmental radio hosts on the planet with her toxic blend of victim-blaming self-help advice and socially conservative commentary. *The Huffington Post* compiled a few of her more alarming statements over the years, which included claiming that being gay is a "biological error that inhibits you from relating normally to the opposite sex" and blaming feminists for destroying "the sanctity of motherhood."

So given her track record of judgment—much of it laid out in books like *The Ten Commandments: The Significance of God's Laws in Everyday Life*—there was more than a little schadenfreude when, in 1998, Schlessingler's former boss Bill Ballance sold nude photos of the radio star from the 1970s to a porn site. The photos were taken while Schlessinger, who was going through a divorce, was involved in a relationship with Ballance, who was married at the time.

Schlessinger sued Ballance unsuccessfully and explained to her audience that she had been a different person in those years and had since repented.

The benefits from my weight loss have been amazing. I sleep better, and since I'm not snoring, my wife sleeps better—which makes for a happier household. . . . And to those guys out there who are happy fat men like I was, certain body parts perform so much better that you'll feel like you're a teenager again.

—Juan-Carlos Cruz, *The Juan-Carlos Cruz Calorie Countdown Cookbook: A 5-Week Eating Strategy for Sustainable Weight Loss*

Judging from obesity statistics, most Americans need some inspiration in their quest to lose weight—and judging from his most recent mug shot, Mr. Cruz has managed to keep the weight off.

It's the happier household part that tripped up the pastry chef turned diet expert. In 2010, he tried to hire three homeless men to murder his wife.

The details of the case are bizarre. TMZ reported, citing law enforcement sources, that Cruz's wife was despondent over her inability to have children and told friends repeatedly about her desire to end her life, but she was unwilling to because of her religion. Cruz's plan, apparently, was to, out of respect for his wife's religious wishes, hire homeless people to kill her; then he would kill himself because his religion offers no such opposition to suicide, and they would be united in heaven. It was a great example of just how functional interdenominational marriages can be, when both parties are willing to make sacrifices for each other.

Cruz will have to wait a little while longer for heaven. He's currently serving a nine-year sentence in a supermax prison in California.

I believe happiness . . . comes when you extend yourself and reach out to others. When you reach out with the loving, caring hand of concern to help someone find their way or to give them a little guidance or support along the way.

—Jerry Sandusky,
Touched: The Jerry Sandusky Story

Jerry Sandusky's 2001 memoir is probably the creepiest book of all time. In a blurb on the back of the book, *Sports Illustrated*'s Jack McCallum noted prophetically that "Here's the best thing you can say about Jerry Sandusky. He's the main reason that Penn State is Linebacker U . . . and linebackers aren't even his enduring legacy."

The book, which became a hot collector's item on eBay in the wake of Sandusky's arrest and conviction on massive quantities of child molestation charges, tells the story of Sandusky's life and career at Penn State—and his foundation the Second Mile, the nonprofit he founded and used to recruit children for his sex acts. In the book's foreword, legendary NFL coach Dick Vermeil writes that Sandusky is "an original piece of work." Future editions of the book might want to replace *work* with a different word.

The single biggest predictor of good results versus bad results is whether kids come from a stable, loving, nurturing, two-parent family. . . . A lot of folks here in Washington don't fully understand that. . . . I am one small example of that progress.

—David Vitter on the floor of the Senate in 2006, supporting a constitutional amendment to define marriage as between a man and a woman

In 2003, Republican congressman David Vitter of Louisiana joined five other congressmen in introducing a constitutional amendment to ban same-sex marriage; he continued to support the measure after his rise to the U.S. Senate. In 2007, he was identified as a patron of prostitutes; his name was on the client list for the D.C. Madam, Deborah Jeane Palfrey. Vitter called his enjoyment of whores a "serious sin" and managed to get reelected in 2010. Unfazed by his hypocrisy, he has stood by his anti-gay, "pro-family" politics. He's also been a big proponent of abstinence-only sex education: "Abstinence education is a public health strategy focused on risk avoidance that aims to help young people avoid exposure to harm . . . by teaching teenagers that saving sex until marriage and remaining faithful afterwards is the best choice for health and happiness," he wrote in 2007.

If Senator Vitter is an example of progress in maintaining family values, we may be in more trouble than he realizes.

Marriage requires some compromises, which you must be willing to make if you love someone.

—Herman Cain, *CEO of Self: You're in Charge*

After Herman Cain wrapped up a successful career as a restaurant executive, he rebranded himself as a motivational speaker and author with books like *CEO of Self: You're in Charge*, *Speak as a Leader: Develop the Better Speaker in You*, and *Leadership Is Common Sense*.

Then in 2012, he ran for the Republican nomination for president of the United States and, ever so briefly, was the front-runner. He was a favorite of the Tea Party set and made an appearance at Glenn Beck's Restoring Courage event. Then allegations of sexual impropriety going back more than a decade surfaced. According to complaints that resulted in settlements, the sacrifices that Cain's wife was required to make included tolerating Cain's sexual harassment of several employees while he was head of the National Restaurant Association. The allegations included groping and unwanted sexual advances. Cain denied all the accusations, but his poll numbers tanked, and he dropped out of the race to become a cable news personality and newsletter writer; his newsletter included an ad for an all-natural erectile dysfunction supplement.

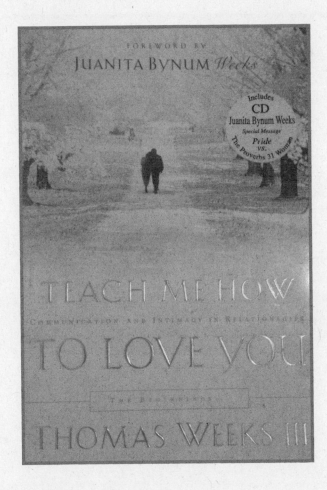

FOREWORD BY
JUANITA BYNUM *Weeks*

Includes
CD
Juanita Bynum Weeks
Special Message
Pride
vs.
The Proverbs 31 Woman

TEACH ME HOW

COMMUNICATION AND INTIMACY IN RELATIONSHIPS

TO LOVE YOU

THE BEGINNINGS

THOMAS WEEKS III

It's not fair to marry a woman and not be concerned with fulfilling her dreams.

—Thomas Weeks III, *Teach Me How to Love You: The Beginnings . . .*

Pentecostal televangelist Thomas Weeks III and his wife, gospel singer Juanita Bynum Weeks, were stars of the Christian media; in addition to their books and TV show, they taught a popular workshop called "Teach Me How to Love You"—which they billed as the "Relationship Conference of the Decade." Their own 2002 wedding had been broadcast live on Trinity Broadcasting Network.

But by August 21, 2007, the marital bliss they'd pontificated on in their 2003 book was gone. Weeks was arrested after an event that involved kicking his wife in a hotel parking lot, which left her with severe bruises. He was initially charged with aggravated assault and making terroristic threats, but he pleaded guilty to a single count of assault and was sentenced to three years' probation, two hundred hours of community service, and anger management classes.

After the couple divorced, Weeks self-published a book in which he blamed their split on Bynum's vanity—"She wanted to be the next Oprah at any cost," he explained—and, apparently, rather than helping her fulfill her dreams, he figured he'd assault her. In 2009, Weeks remarried; only this time, instead of touting his relationship as a model for others, he wisely opted for a quiet ceremony with a honeymoon to an undisclosed location. Weeks is currently busy rebuilding his ministry and reputation with books like *Millionaires Don't Go to Sleep Without Brushing Their Teeth: How to Awaken the Millionaire Within*. Another great bit of advice.

I want to help ANYONE ANYWHERE that I can while knowing that the time and resources I've been given will responsibly be put to use. Naturally, we're most capable of helping those whom we've come into contact with.

—Tim Lambesis, on his personal blog, *TIMLAMBESIS*

As the front man of the popular Christian heavy metal band As I Lay Dying, thirty-three-year-old Tim Lambesis had everything he could possibly want—and, apparently, a wife he didn't. So he went in search of someone willing to help him with the same devotion he used to help others. On May 7, 2013, he was arrested after he allegedly tried to hire an undercover cop to kill her. Through a contact at his gym—his lawyer blamed steroid abuse for Lambesis's odd behavior—he handed an officer (code name "Red") an envelope with one thousand dollars in cash, along with pictures of his wife, the code to get into the gated community where she lived, and the date he wanted her killed. "Just to clarify, just so you know . . . I do want her dead," the undercover officer testified Lambesis told him. As of mid-2013, Lambesis was out on bail awaiting trial for one count of solicitation of murder. He faces nine years in prison.

We need to learn to have realistic expectations and let people off the hook. By giving people room to be human, we can avoid a lot of heartache.

—Victoria Osteen, *Love Your Life: Living Happy, Healthy & Whole*

In her *New York Times* bestselling book, the wife and copastor of megachurch pastor Joel Osteen offered inspirational tips on how to live a better life by loving yourself and then extending that compassion to others.

She also likes metaphors.

"If you have ever flown in a commercial airplane, then you have heard the flight attendant's instructions, informing passengers about airplane exits, emergency lighting, flotation devices, and oxygen masks that fall from above your head in case the cabin loses pressure," she writes. "Then the flight attendant will say something like this: 'Place the oxygen mask over your nose and mouth before assisting children or those around you.'"

Ms. Osteen apparently took good notes on that part of the airline safety lecture—but ignored the part about obeying the instructions of crew members.

In December 2005, Ms. Osteen, her husband, and their children boarded a Continental Airlines flight for a ski vacation in Vail, Colorado. An altercation ensued after Ms. Osteen became distressed about liquid spilled on the armrest of her first-class seat. "She was just abusive," one passenger told a reporter of Ms. Osteen's behavior. "She was just like one of those divas."

"This is ridiculous. I'm a first-class passenger," the self-help author whose chapters included "Embracing What's Important" and "Keeping the Right Perspective" reportedly bellowed.

In a civil suit, flight attendant Sharon Brown accused Ms. Osteen of throwing her against a bathroom door and elbowing her in the left breast. Eventually, according to the Federal Aviation Administration, Ms. Osteen and her family were asked to leave the plane, resulting in a two-and-a-half-hour delay. Ms. Osteen denied the physical aspect of the altercation, and a jury sided with her when Brown filed a lawsuit. She did pay the FAA's fine of three thousand dollars.

Being in rapport is the ability to enter someone else's model of the world and let them know that we truly understand their model. And it's letting someone come into our frame of the world and having an experience of them truly understanding us.

—Michael Brooks, *Instant Rapport*

The 1989 book *Instant Rapport* is a horribly written, gobbledygook-laden guide to neurolinguistic programming written by "industrial psychologist and nationally acclaimed communications expert" Michael Brooks. Nevertheless, it became a bestseller on the strength of plugs from Oprah and Sally Jessy Raphael.

On June 28, 1999, Brooks called the DA's office in the Bronx to check up on charges he was pressing against his neighbor, who had allegedly slashed the tires on his Jeep as part of an ongoing feud.

When Brooks didn't get the information he wanted from the paralegal who answered the phone, he sought to build rapport. "I will get a gun and shoot you . . . because you don't know what the fuck you are doing with this case," he said, according to the harassment complaint. According to the *New York Post*, "Brooks was arrested again on Aug. 24 for allegedly driving off with two brand-new tires from a Bronx tire shop without paying. In that case, he was charged with petit larceny, theft of services and possessing stolen property."

A month prior to that, he was arrested for flashing a counterfeit U.S. marshal's badge in an altercation with the crew on a plane and eventually sentenced to two years' probation and ordered to continue undergoing psychiatric treatment. He has not made headlines since.

Sometimes people may say, 'He's off his rocker . . . he doesn't drink, he doesn't run around with women, he doesn't cuss . . . he's weird.'. . . I . . . think there is extreme value in refraining from some things.

—Chad Curtis

Chad Curtis played ten seasons of Major League Baseball, and even though he never became a superstar, he put up solid numbers with the Angels, Tigers, and Yankees in the '90s and early 2000s.

But he was most famous for his occasionaly obnoxious devotion to his Christian faith—and his desire to tell his teammates all about it. He once enraged teammate Royce Clayton in the locker room by turning down his boom box on the grounds that rap music was immoral. His proslytizing to Jewish teammate Gabe Kapler was so incessant that, at wit's end, Kapler called his agent, Paul Cohen (whom the *Jewish Journal* described as a "a kippah-wearing Jew") for advice. Cohen arranged what turned into a three-hour dinner meeting at a kosher restaurant with Curtis, Kapler, and a rabbi.

"Do me a favor," the rabbi told Curtis. "Let the Jewish people find God in their own way."

Curtis laid off Kapler but remained unconvinced.

"If I have something that I believe is the truth and it's necessary for other people to come to some type of a recognition or grip of that truth then I want to share it," he once told ESPN.

Post-retirement, Curtis's faith wasn't the only thing he couldn't keep to himself.

In 2012, Curtis, a married volunteer strength trainer at Lakewood High School in Michigan, was charged with inapropriate sexual touching of three girls between the ages of fifteen and sixteen. In all, he was charged with five counts of criminal sexual conduct. In court testimony, one girl charged that Curtis, under the guise of helping with a hip injury, took off her clothes in a locked, windowless weight room. He also allegedly pulled up a sports bra and rubbed a girl's breasts—despite no reports of a chest injury. He was convicted of sexual abuse in October 2013 and sentenced to seven to fifteen years in prison.

Violence is not a game. No one ever wins. If you value something, then you will cherish and preserve it. There are better ways to relieve stress and frustration than to hurt someone. Listen to the other person when he or she tells you that your words and actions hurt them. Do not confuse fear with submission and control with masculinity.

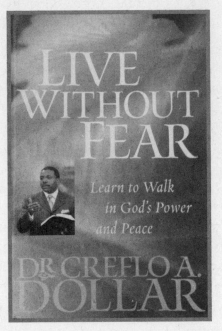

—Dr. Creflo A. Dollar, *The Successful Family: Everything You Need to Know to Build a Stronger Family*

Dr. Creflo A. Dollar—whose only doctorate is an honorary one from Oral Roberts University—is one of the most financially successful televangelists of the modern era. Dollar's ministry took in sixty-nine million dollars in revenue in 2006 alone—some of it coming from books with preposterously ambitious titles—and MinistryWatch gave his organization an F in financial transparency.

On June 8, 2012, he was arrested in Fayetteville, Georgia, for attacking his fifteen-year-old daughter during an argument about whether she could attend a party. Dollar's nineteen-year-old daughter said she watched her father "put both hands around her sister's neck and [choke] her for about five seconds," according to the police report. Dollar then allegedly threw his daughter on the ground, slapped her, and beat her with a shoe. The next time he spoke to his congregation, he was greeted with a rousing display of support—and explained that the marks on his daughter's throat were eczema-related as parishioners shouted "Amen," and he attributed the incident to Satan's effort to "discredit" his ministry.

The charges were dropped after he agreed to anger management counseling that included regular meetings with a probation officer, and his new book, *The Holy Spirit, Your Financial Advisor: God's Plan for Debt-Free Money Management*, was released in 2013. He can be seen regularly on the Trinity Broadcasting Network.

We must never forget this.
Anything that tends to debase
the human body or pervert it is
wrong, sinful, and wicked.

—Jimmy Swaggart,
Questions & Answers: Bible-Based Answers
to Your Questions About Life

Jimmy Swaggart's 1985 book was conservative and moralistic even by the standards of right-wing moralist conservatives. He explains his opposition to public swimming pools and writes that "[A]ll dancing, by whatever name it may be called, is sinful and harmful"—including aerobic dancing. Christians should "avoid all movies."

"Can we, in good conscience, spend our money to help some jaded actor or actress pay alimony to his fourth or fifth wife (or husband)?" he asks. "I think not. Our money is far too valuable to waste in such a way."

Oral sex between husband and wife is also verboten.

Yes, sir, all *you* need is Jesus. Swaggart might have needed Jesus, but he also wanted hookers. And his 1988 televised apology is still one of the most famous televised apologies of all time: "I have sinned against You, my Lord," he said, never specifically noting what his sin had been. "And I would ask that Your Precious Blood would wash and cleanse every stain until it is in the seas of God's forgiveness, not to be remembered against me anymore," he cried.

In 1991, Swaggart was back in the news—with his second john bust. "He asked me for sex. I mean, that's why he stopped me. That's what I do. I'm a prostitute," Rosemary Garcia helpfully told the police officer who pulled the pair over. "The Lord told me it's flat none of your business," Swaggart told his congregation of the incident.

These days, Swaggart is still providing moral leadership. Jimmy Swaggart Ministries continues to broadcast its weekly show on seventy-eight channels in more than a hundred countries.

On his Facebook page, Swaggart shared a note written by his grandson Gabriel that ripped into the Harlem Shake dance craze: "It saddens me deeply seeing the nonsense that is going on the Church today. With the leadership of the Church heading in the wrong direction, allowing the stupidity of the 'Harlem Shake,' the playing of secular music from behind our pulpits, the Church has resorted to an all out flesh party"—something Swaggart normally enjoys.

When you reach out in love, don't expect anything in return. But you are going to get something in return because what you sow, you will reap.

—JimBakker, *Eight Keys to Success*

At its peak, Bakker's television ministiry PTL (Praise the Lord) took in $129 million per year in revenue—and with Jim Bakker and his wife, Tammy Faye, hocking a $675 doll modeled after Tammy on air, why not? Their Heritage USA resort drew six million visitors per year, making it the most popular non-Disney resort destination in America. But it didn't enter the consciousness of the secular world until the Bakker's ministry imploded under the weight of virtually every type of scandal imaginable: embezzlement, crooked pledge drives, extramarital affairs, Tammy Faye's trip to the Betty Ford Center to battle an Ativan addiction, gold faucets, and, of course, an air-conditioned doghouse financed by the donations of viewers.

And what church scandal would be complete without allegations of homosexuality? Jay Babcock, PTL's former director of creative television, testified before a grand jury that he had had sex with Bakker. In his defense, Bakker offered one of the most self-serving examples of illeism in history: "If people can't forgive Jim and Tammy, then the whole world is doomed to hell."

When Jerry Falwell—that bastion of charity and forgiveness—took over the ministry, he called Jim Bakker "probably the greatest scab and cancer on the face of Christianity in two thousand years of church history."

Bakker served close to five years in federal prison, where he cleaned toilets. He still owes the IRS six million dollars in back taxes—but he's not letting that stop him. Like any self-respecting, washed-up red state icon, he's got his own theater in Branson, Missouri, where he still tapes his own TV show every day. His latest book contains his apocalyptic prophesies, and if you believe what you read, the Love Gifts section on his Web page has everything you need to prepare. For your donation of three thousand dollars, you can buy Bakker's Time of Trouble & Survival Too end-times preparation kit—which includes, among other things, "forty-two 200 Serving Limited Edition Emergency Food Buckets."

If the basic reason for sexual intimacy is simply to satisfy that physical desire, sex becomes legalized masturbation. . . . Sexual desire alone never produces true integration of two people into one spirit.

—Earl Paulk, *Sex Is God's Idea*

Even by the standards of 1980s televangelists, Earl Paulk was a horndog. As the founder of the megachurch Cathedral at Chapel Hill in Decatur, Georgia, Paulk was a progressive in many ways: he opened his church to African Americans years before most others did, and in the last years of his ministry, he made headlines for welcoming gays and lesbians.

His 1985 book *Sex Is God's Idea* preached the benefits of godly sexuality—embracing the pleasures of sexuality within the confines of a traditional monogamous marriage with each person as an equal partner.

In his own life, Paulk failed to live up to his standard of godly sexuality, becoming embroiled in more sex scandals than just about anyone. In 1992, six women accused him of sexual impropriety. In 2001, a former parishioner sued him, alleging molestation when she was in elementary school; that suit was settled for four hundred thousand dollars. In 2007, his nephew Donnie Earl Paulk, by then the senior pastor of the church, revealed that he actually wasn't Earl Paulk's nephew; he was his son, according to a DNA test. Earl Paulk had had an affair with his sister-in-law. That's just a few of the Earl Paulk scandals that we know about. He should have stuck with masturbation.

Insensitive assertion and promiscuous conquest are spurious stereotypes of masculinity. A true male identity is reflected in the caring and protective role of the responsible father and husband.

—George Alan Rekers, *Shaping Your Child's Sexual Identity*

Dr. George Alan Rekers was the head of the Department of Family and Child Development at Kansas State University. He's most prominent as an advocate for the notion that sexual orientation can be changed through therapy and for his belief that gay couples cannot make good parents.

His book *Shaping Your Child's Sexual Identity* is terrifying in its brutality. In a case study, he writes of a five-year-old who walked in an effeminate manner and was more interested in playing with girl toys than boy toys. Dr. Rekers reports that, through a regimen that included rewards for acting masculine and spankings for playing with girl toys, under his supervision, the child's parents were able to cure the child of his propensity for effeminate behavior. In 2008, the state of Florida paid Rekers $120,000 for his expert witness testimony against the idea of allowing gay couples to adopt children.

Dr. Rekers's methods may have been less successful in his own life. On May 6, 2010, the *Miami New Times* reported that three weeks prior, the sixty-two-year-old had been photographed at Miami International Airport with Jo-Vanni Roman, a twenty-year-old hustler he had found on RentBoy .com.

"If you talk with my travel assistant . . . you will find I spent a great deal of time sharing scientific information on the desirability of abandoning homosexual intercourse, and I shared the Gospel of Jesus Christ with him in great detail," Rekers explained. The hustler, however, said that Rekers had paid him for daily nude massages that included genital contact. Seven days after the story broke, Dr. Rekers, who denied the allegations, resigned from the board of directors for the National Association for Research & Therapy of Homosexuality. He now has more time to devote to his role of protective and responsible father and husband; they are doubtless delighted to have him to themselves now that the demand for his expert witness testimony and gay reparative therapy seems to have softened.

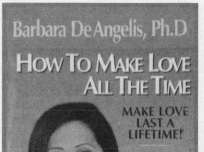

Underneath all unpleasant emotions is love and the desire for connection.

—Barbara De Angelis, *How to Make Love All the Time: Make Love Last a Lifetime!*

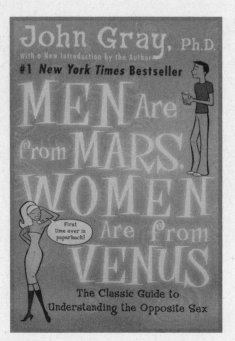

To forget her own painful feelings a woman may become emotionally involved in the problems of others.

—John Gray, *Men Are from Mars, Women Are from Venus*

What happens when two number one *New York Times* bestselling relationship experts—she with *Are You the One for Me?: Knowing Who's Right & Avoiding Who's Wrong* and he with *Men Are from Mars, Women Are from Venus: The Classic Guide to Understanding the Opposite Sex*—marry each other?

If you guessed a lifetime of lawfully wedded bliss, you haven't been paying attention to the theme of this book.

After two years, Barbara De Angelis, PhD, and John Gray, PhD (both were later exposed as having earned their degrees from diploma mills), divorced. Gray later said that he came up with the idea for *Men Are from Mars, Women Are from Venus* while watching *E.T.* and bragged that one of his books took just seven weeks to write. "I feel it's in me to help negotiate peace in the world," he once told *Time* magazine. "I know it will happen one day." So far it hasn't, but he has followed his original hit with *Mars and Venus on a Date*, *Mars and Venus Together Forever*, *Mars and Venus in the Bedroom*, *Mars and Venus Starting Over*, *Mars and Venus in Love*, *Children Are from Heaven*, *How to Get What You Want at Work*, *Practical Miracles for Mars & Venus*, *How to Get What You Want and Want What You Have*, and *The Mars & Venus Diet & Exercise Solution*.

Post-divorce but mid-relationship expert career, a reader asked De Angelis what she thought of Gray's work in an online chat. She responded in Internet-speak: "Does any-one listening know that I was married to him 20 years ago? LOL Needless to say we're divorced. Does that answer your question? I'm from earth." She then joked that a chat with him could have been called "Mars Attacks."

PART SIX

KEEP THE FAITH (OUT OF WEDLOCK), BABY

Religious leadership and hypocrisy go together like inspirational athletes and illegal drugs.

Pulpits attract narcissists, and when their followers demand that they provide weekly moral pronouncements, irony often ensues. For years, one of the most inspiring religious leaders was a preteen named Marjoe Gortner, who, under the direction of his stage mother, made millions during the 1940s and 1950s as a traveling boy-wonder evangelist. His sermons sold well as records, with messages like this one, delivered when he was eight years old: "I say hell is a place of extreme bodily suffering. . . . In hell, you'll be oh so lonely. People say 'Oh, there'll be plenty of company in hell.' But they'll be [so] taken up with their own suffering and their own shame that they'll not care a thing about you." Later, he renounced his charlatanism and starred in an Academy Award–winning documentary, *Marjoe*, where he exposed the tricks of his trade.

Still: He wasn't there to trash faith. He just wanted people to see through the leaders they put too much trust in. "I hope that they will see it's not necessary to look to some person to, like, jerk you off," he said of his goals in making the film.

God's business is the greatest and most important business in the world. As pastors, we have a responsibility to see that His business is managed properly—at least as well as we would manage a secular enterprise.

—Marvin Gorman, *Called to Victory: How to Succeed as a Pastor*

In 1982, Marvin Gorman published *Called to Victory: How to Succeed as a Pastor*. In it he offered advice on everything it took be a successful pastor, including twenty-two pages on "Church Administration and Budget."

Five years later, Gorman and his church were both bankrupt. Marvin Gorman Ministries reported more than two million dollars in debt according to the Associated Press, and Gorman and his wife had another six hundred thousand dollars of their own liabilities.

The bankruptcy petition was filed two weeks after a judge threw out Gorman's ninety-million-dollar lawsuit against fellow televangelist Jimmy Swaggart, who had accused the pastor of patronizing prostitutes. Gorman had admitted to infidelity, and the scandal led to declining revenues at his church—although there were already financial issues prior to Swaggart's attacks.

Happily, Gorman got his revenge: he hired his son and son-in-law to stake out a dive motel where Jimmy Swaggart engaged in his own dalliances with hookers. Using a camera with a telephoto lens draped with a black cloth, they caught Swaggart in the act. When Swaggart failed to live up to his promise to work to have Gorman's ministry restored in exchange for keeping the photos private, Gorman went to the Assemblies of God oversight organization with the photos—leading to Swaggart's fall.

Normal financial planning in God's economy is to ask Him first and not worry about anything else. . . . If God can give birds feathers and nests and seeds . . . He can pretty much take care of anything I might need. In the natural, worry is normal, but not in the spiritual realm.

—Stephen Baldwin, *The Unusual Suspect: My Calling to the New Hardcore Movement of Faith*

Baldwin, to his credit, practices what he preaches and has on more than one occasion proven his trust that God will take care of everything: like when he failed to file income taxes for three years.

Of course that doesn't mean that this washed up actor turned Christian crusader doesn't occasionally rely on human intervention. In 2012, he went to court with Kevin Costner, whom he accused of cheating him out of millions of dollars on an investment in an oil clean-up invention. The jury took less than two hours to award him nothing. He now does radio commercials for teeth whitening—exactly as Jesus would have.

You'll never make the right choices as long as you shudder and stay safe inside the boat. Get out. Take a risk. Trust Jesus' strong arms to grab you if you begin to fall.

—Bishop Eddie Long

I t was megachurch bishop Eddie Long's strong arms that got him into trouble in the first place. In 2010, he was accused of sending pictures of those strong arms that he'd taken in gym locker rooms to young adults he was mentoring; those pictures quickly surfaced on the Internet. Four lawsuits accusing Long of sexual improprieties were filed, alleging coercion involving expensive gifts, luxury travel, and oral sex. One lawsuit alleged that Long would "discuss the Holy Scripture to justify and support the sexual activity." Long denied all the charges.

The suits were ultimately settled out of court, and Long continues to preach the antigay gospel that had led the Southern Poverty Law Center to call him, in 2007, "one of the most virulently homophobic black leaders in the religiously based anti-gay movement."

Long has managed to keep his lucrative position as senior pastor at New Birth Missionary Baptist Church, but his broader cultural influence has receded. His once popular 2002 book, *What a Man Wants, What a Woman Needs: The Secret to Successful, Fulfilling Relationships,* is now out of print. But he continues on as a pastor and regularly posts inspirational messages on Facebook.

The Christian life leads to health and stable living. Most of us can attest to that from our experience with Christ.

—Anita Bryant, *Light My Candle*

Once a popular recording artist, beauty queen, and spokeswoman for the Florida Citrus Commission, Anita Bryant flushed her career down the toilet in the late 1970s when she engaged in a Christianity-inspired jihad against gays and lesbians. "If gays are granted rights, next we'll have to give rights to prostitutes and to people who sleep with St. Bernards and to nail biters," she said.

In 1980, she got divorced—which extinguished her revenue from the Christian market that was sustaining her ailing career. In her divorce papers, she said she was "without sufficient funds" to support her four children; she also asked to be allowed to use the family's twenty-five-room mansion in Miami Beach until it could be sold.

Since then, she has made several efforts to relaunch her career with theaters in Pigeon Forge, Tennessee, and Branson, Missouri—and bankruptcies, tax problems, and disgruntled and unpaid former employees have followed her. In a 1980 interview with *Ladies' Home Journal*, she backed away from her extremist views, taking a position she probably should have taken about her own religious values back when she still had a career: "I'm more inclined to say live and let live, just don't flaunt it or try to legalize it."

Although it is important to recognize that children are born in a state of sin and are moral beings capable of actual sins against God and others . . . infants and young children are not as sinful as adults and therefore need to be treated tenderly. They do not need as much help to love God and neighbor.

—From *Children's Spirituality: Christian Perspectives, Research, and Applications*, edited by Donald Ratcliff

Wheaton College professor Donald Ratcliff was an expert on religion and children; he taught a class on children's spirituality and authored and edited books like *ChildFaith*: *Experiencing God and Spiritual Growth with Your Children*; *Children's Spirituality: Christian Perspectives, Research, and Applications*; and *Child-Rearing & Personality Development*.

Then he was arrested in 2012 with a massive cache of child pornography. Professor Ratcliff told police that the kiddie porn was "potentially therapeutic" and a "healthy alternative" to adult pornography. Wheaton fired him, and in August 2013 he pleaded guilty, facing up to seven years in prison.

CONCLUSION

WHO IS THE NEXT GOOD ADVISOR
TO BE EXPOSED AS A BAD PERSON?

The work on this book consisted of the most rigorous research into the psychology and methodology of hypocrisy ever conducted. Endless late-night Google News archives searches for phrases like "inspirational icon was arrested" and "bankrupt wealth-building expert" have helped me notice some points of similarity between all—or at least most—people who say one thing and then do something different.

So how can you spot the star of the next edition of *Good Advice from Bad People* before he's been publicly exposed? Here are a few warning signs:

He's a man. It's not that women are superior to men; in lots of ways, they can be just as bad. But there's a certain level of hypocrisy that women just don't seem willing to stoop to. A woman might very well run her company into the ground; she just won't give speeches about how to be an amazing leader while she does it.

He very earnestly tells people about the importance of doing things most people know intuitively. Most of us basically know that greed is dangerous, that violence isn't a good way to solve problems with a spouse, and that it's good to have your heart in the right place. So if you see someone who passionately believes that other people need to be lectured about these things, you should know that he's probably dealing with some internal conflict that most people don't face.

Everyone praises him, but no one really knows anything about him. Enron's a classic example of this: lauded by every analyst as an incredible innovator led by brilliant management, even though no one could really explain how it made its money. Lots of inspirational stories with little specifics on what someone has actually done and how he's done it should be a red flag: he just might be completely full of crap.

He milks it. If an "expert" pumps out product, much of it similar to stuff he's already produced, you should know that you're dealing with a money-grubbing huckster and probably not someone with a sincere desire to help people.

So who is the next annoyingly perfect hero of unimpeachable goodness and integrity to screw up and land in volume two of *Good Advice from Bad People*? It would be irresponsible to speculate but . . . Tim Tebow.

FOR FURTHER WISDOM . . .

The bulk of these books are, quite rightly, long out-of-print—and the better-managed libraries have gracefully removed them from circulation. But they live on at Amazon.com, where nearly all can be had for a penny each plus shipping.

Books

Bakker, Jim. *Eight Keys to Success*. Charlotte, NC: PTL Television Network, 1980.

Baldwin, Stephen. *The Unusual Suspect: My Calling to the New Hardcore Movement of Faith*. New York: FaithWords, 2006.

The Beardstown Ladies Investment Club, with Robin Dellabough. *The Beardstown Ladies' Little Book of Investment Wisdom*. New York: Hyperion, 1997.

Bennett, William J. *The Book of Man: Readings on the Path to Manhood*. Nashville, TN: Thomas Nelson, 2011.

Bloch, H. I. Sonny, and Jerome L. Hollingsworth. *Sonny Bloch's Cover Your Assets*. New York: Perigee Books, 1992.

Brooks, Michael. *Instant Rapport*. New York: Warner Books, 1989.

Bryant, Anita, and Bob Green. *Light My Candle*. Old Tappan, NJ: Revell, 1974.

Canseco, Jose, and Dave McKay. *Strength Training for Baseball*. New York: Perigee, 1990.

FOR FURTHER WISDOM . . .

Cook, Wade. *Wade Cook's Power Quotes*. Seattle: Lighthouse Publishing, 1998.

Cruz, Juan-Carlos. *The Juan-Carlos Cruz Calorie Countdown Cookbook: A 5-Week Eating Strategy for Sustainable Weight Loss*. New York: Gotham Books, 2006.

Cutaia, Susan, and Anthony Cutaia, with Robert Slater. *Untapped Riches: Never Pay Off Your Mortgage—and Other Surprising Secrets for Building Wealth*. New York: AMACOM, 2007.

D'Annunzio, Steve, and Jeff Locker. *Teachings for a New World*. New York: White Light Press, 1998.

De Angelis, Barbara. *How to Make Love All the Time: Make Love Last a Lifetime!* New York: Dell, 1991.

Dollar, Creflo A., and Taffi L. Dollar. *The Successful Family: Everything You Need to Know to Build a Stronger Family*. College Park, GA: Creflo Dollar Ministries, 2004.

Dunlap, Albert J., with Bob Andelman. *Mean Business: How I Save Bad Companies and Make Good Companies Great*. New York: Crown Business, 1996.

Fortino, Michael. *e-Mergency*. Palmdale, CA: Omni, 2001.

Garlington, Ernest C. *Roots of a Man: 7 Principles For Growing Strong and Powerful*. Charleston, SC: BookSurge Publishing, 2005.

Gingrich, Newt, and Jackie Gingrich Cushman. *5 Principles for a Successful Life: From Our Family to Yours*. New York: Crown Forum, 2009.

Givens, Charles J. *Super Self: Doubling Your Personal Effectiveness*. New York: Simon & Schuster, 1993.

Gorman, Marvin. *Called to Victory: How to Succeed as a Pastor*. New Orleans: Marvin Gorman Ministries, 1982.

Gray, John. *Men Are from Mars, Women Are from Venus*. New York: HarperCollins, 1993.

Haggard, Ted, and Gayle Haggard. *From This Day Forward: Making Your Vows Last a Lifetime*. Colorado Springs: Water Brook Press, 2006.

Holyfield, Evander, with Lee Gruenfeld. *Becoming Holyfield: A Fighter's Journey*. New York: Atria Books, 2008.

Jackson Jr., Jesse. *It's About the Money!: How You Can Get Out of Debt, Build Wealth, and Achieve Your Financial Dreams.* New York: Times Business, 1999.

Kelleher, Paul, and Rebecca van der Boger, eds. *Voices for Democracy: Struggles and Celebrations of Transformational Leaders*. Chicago: National Society for the Study of Education, 2006.

Lay, Kenneth L. *The Enron Story*. New York: Newcomen Society of the United States, 1990.

Lehrer, Jonah. *Imagine: How Creativity Works*. New York: Houghton Mifflin Harcourt, 2012.

Long, Eddie L., and Cecil Murphey. *60 Seconds to Greatness: Seize the Moment and Plan for Success*. New York: Berkley Praise, 2010.

McNamara, Robert S. *The Essence of Security: Reflections in Office*. New York: Harper & Row, 1968.

Minkow, Barry. *Making It in America: 18 Years Old and a Million Dollars*. Los Angeles: B. Minkow, 1985.

Morris, Dick. *The New Prince: Machiavelli Updated for the Twenty-First Century*. New York: Renaissance Books, 1999.

Nixon, Richard M. *Six Crises*. New York: Doubleday, 1962.

Osteen, Victoria. *Love Your Life: Living Happy, Healthy, and Whole*. New York: Howard Books, 2009.

Pearlman, Lou, with Wes Smith. *Bands, Brands, & Billions: My Top 10 Rules for Making Any Business Go Platinum*. New York: McGraw-Hill, 2003.

Pettitte, Andy, and Bob Reccord, with Mark Tabb. *Strike Zone: Targeting a Life of Integrity & Purity*. Nashville, TN: B&H Books, 2005.

Ratcliff, Donald, ed. *Children's Spirituality: Christian Perspectives, Research, and Applications*. Eugene, OR: Wipf & Stock Publishers, 2004.

Rekers, George Alan. *Shaping Your Child's Sexual Identity*. Grand Rapids, MI: Baker Book House, 1982.

Rumseld, Donald. *Rumsfeld's Rules*. New York: Broadside Books, 2013.

Sandusky, Jerry. *Touched: The Jerry Sandusky Story*. Champaign, IL: Sports Publishing LLC, 2001.

Schlessinger, Laura. *Ten Stupid Things Men Do to Mess Up Their Lives*. New York: Harper Perennial, 2002.

Schuller, Robert H. *Hours of Power: My Daily Book of Motivation and Inspiration*. New York: HarperOne, 2004.

Sculley, John, and John A. Byrne. *Odyssey: Pepsi to Apple . . . A Journey of Adventure, Ideas and the Future*. New York: Harper & Rowe, 1987.

Shawkey, Gary. *If I Can . . . Anybody Can . . .* Mechanicsville, VA: International, Inc., 2003.

FOR FURTHER WISDOM . . .

Swaggart, Jimmy. *Questions & Answers: Bible-Based Answers to Your Questions About Life*. Baton Rouge, LA: Swaggart Ministries, 1985.

Thompson, Carolyn B., and Jim Ware. *The Leadership Genius of George W. Bush: 10 Common Sense Lessons from the Commander in Chief*. New York: Wiley, 2002.

Trump, Donald, with Charles Leerhsen. *Trump: Surviving at the Top*. New York: Random House, 1990.

Weeks, Thomas. *Teach Me How to Love You: The Beginnings . . .* Denver, CO: Legacy Publishers International, 2003.

Weiner, Michael A. *The Complete Book of Homeopathy: A Comprehensive Manual of Natural Healing*. New York: Avery, 1998.

Whitmore, Kay R. *A Common Agenda for an Uncommon Future: Addressed to the Sloan School of Management*. Cambridge, MA: Ulan Press, 2012.

Videos and Other Multimedia

Fuld, Richard. Commencement speech at the University of Colorado at Boulder. Delivered on May 12, 2006. Available online at http://commencement.colorado.edu/speeches/past-commencement-speeches-2006.

"Nobel laureate Myron Scholes Discusses Risk in Management," YouTube video, 10:43, posted by "SmithBusinessSchool," November 29, 2010, http://www.youtube.com/watch?v=90SqsRqnVxA.

"Ron Johnson," YouTube video, 39:97, from Ron Johnson's speech at Stanford University School of Medicine, posted by "stanfordmedicine," June 12, 2012, http://www.youtube.com/watch?v=pVt8tHeCrIU.